Presented To:

_____

From:

_____

Date:

_____

YOU are like no other woman in the world.
YOU are unique and you hold tremendous power.

BUILT TO PROSPER FOR WOMEN

Built To Prosper For Women

The 9 Principles of Self-Mastery

Deborah Francis
&
Hasheem Francis

Copyright © 2016 by Built To Prosper University. All rights reserved. Distribution and reproduction are strictly prohibited by law.

All Scriptures are from the King James Version unless otherwise noted.

No part of this publication may be reproduced, stored in a retrieval system, or transmitted in any form, or by any means: electronic mechanical, photocopying, recorded, scanning, or otherwise, except as permitted under Section 107 or 108 of the 1976 United States Copyright Act without the prior written permission of the publisher or authors.

All request to the authors should be addressed to BTP Publishing Group LLC at info@BTPPublish.com.

For information about reprints rights, translation, or bulk purchases, please contact Deborah Francis at info@BTPPublish.com or you may write to BTP Publishing Group, LLC at P.O. Box 552, Plymouth, FL 32768 for visit **www.BTPPublish.com**.

Built To Prosper For Women; The 9 Principles of Self-Mastery
Authors: Deborah Francis & Hasheem Francis
Cover designed by: BTP Marketing Group
Edited by: BTP Marketing Group
ISBN: 978-0615541532
Published by: BTP Publishing Group. Plymouth, FL

DEDICATION

To our two beautiful daughters, India and Savannah, you are destined for greatness. Both of you are leaders in your own right.

Also to the future generation, may the thoughts in this book inspire you to achieve all that your heart desires. Lastly, to every woman who has the ambition to be all that God created you to be, you are definitely Built To Prosper.

CONTENTS

ACKNOWLEDGEMENTS……………………….........	13
INTRODUCTION………………………………………..	15
THE FOUNDATION…………………………………....	23
CHAPTER I - I Am What I Think I Am………………….	49
CHAPTER II - Guard Your Mouth………………………..	61
CHAPTER III - My Attitude is Either My Friend or Foe…	73
CHAPTER IV - Whose Report Do You Believe?.................	87
CHAPTER V - Creating an Inspired Vision………………..	97
CHAPTER VI - Decide or Be Conformed…….…………..	115
CHAPTER VII - Are You Committed to the Cause?..........	121
CHAPTER VIII - Creating Your Circle of Trust…………..	131
CHAPTER IX - I Shall Have What I Desire……………...	147
CHAPTER X - What To Do Now? Take Action…..……..	159
BIBLIOGRAPHY…………………………………………...	193
ABOUT THE AUTHORS………………………………....	195
RECOMMENDED READING LIST…………………….	197

"Be a great student of life, so you can be an outstanding teacher of living." Hasheem Francis

Mentors Help YOU Excel to the Next Level!

It is a fact that most people who are mentors do it because they LOVE helping others! They love working with someone and helping them get from where they are to where they want to be, bringing out their best, helping them think bigger, fostering those big breakthroughs, etc. **Built To Prosper Mentoring Program remains the most comprehensive program of its kind and a leader's best choice for exceeding their maximum goals.**

If you are highly motivated and want the individualized or corporate mentoring by one of our true experts, then you need our mentoring program. Our mentors specialize in giving you the latest techniques on how to build a profitable business, become an effective leader, amass wealth, and develop a healthy lifestyle.

Built To Prosper Mentoring focuses on 4 areas: Business, Leadership, Wealth and Health. Mentoring enables you to reach your full potential in life.

It gives you the ability to promote your personal and professional development in a strategic and supportive way, leading to enhanced returns on your investment.

Visit us at: www.BTPMentoring.com

ACKNOWLEDGEMENTS

Many have helped influence this body of work. I am deeply grateful for every woman who has inspired and encouraged me through their written word or through their presence.

I would like to acknowledge and express my gratitude to all the mentors, past and present teachers, business partners, friends, and family members who have guided me throughout my journey.

Special thanks to all the women who have shared their God-given gift with the world: Ludel Black, Dorothy Johnson, Amoceita Beckford, Lascena Upkpong, Maya Angelou, Oprah Winfrey, Kim Kiyosaki, Catherine Ponder, Sharon Lechter, Mary Kay, Debra L. Lee, Peggy McColl, Lori Langmeyer, Iyanla Vanzant, Michelle Obama, Angela Davis, Toni Morrison, Alice Walker, Madame CJ Walker, Condoleezza Rice, Jane Austen, Emily Dickinson, and every phenomenal woman who stood in the gap and paved the way.

Thanks to the following organizations who develop the resources that help other women achieve greatness: W.O.S.A. (Women of Sovereign Authority), Women of Wisdom, The Women's Conference, Women of Faith, The Rich Woman Company, Cashology Academy, Extraordinary Women, Millionaire University, Enlightened Wealth Institute, Rich Life Investments, LLC., Success Inc., Mary Kay, Life Success Productions, The Joy of Healthy Living, Pay Your Family First.

INTRODUCTION

> "If you try to "open the eyes" of someone "who does not want to see" they are going to despise you in the end. You may not be able to change the world you see around you, but you can change what you see within YOU." Deborah Francis

We would like to commend you for investing in yourself; within this wonderful experience we call life, you reap what you sow. This book is a complete guide on building the life you truly desire. We know that is a bold claim to make. The only way to know if these claims are true is through results. We have seen, firsthand that these principles have changed many women's lives. As parents of two daughters, we have a vested interest in helping women live a prosperous life. The intention of this book is to help you take an inward journey to understand what you need in your life to be successful and prosperous. The only authentic power we have lies with us – and out attitude toward life. The primary driver for women is the desire to do work that matters. You were born to lead an empowered life.

"If a young woman looks upward and sees few or no leaders she can relate to, she may never see leadership as a believable future for her or other women." - Deborah Francis

A woman who succeeds in life must know where she is going and settle within her mind, with an unshakable faith, that she is indeed capable of achieving her goals no matter how distant the destination. You must seize the moment and make it happen, because power and success come from creating your own destiny. Most of my life, I have studied different systems and applied life changing principles to get the results I desired.

What I have found, and my mentor expressed to me is "success leaves clues." In the earlier stages of my development, I thought I knew it all, I let my ego get in the way of my success. It was when I became coachable that I began to understand and apply the principles of success. I discovered that prosperity is not just financial blessings. Prosperity also includes peace, wisdom, favor, success, good health and every good thing you could possibly need—all the wonderful things God desires for you to have. **God's will is for you to prosper in spirit, soul and body.** Without peace of mind, life is just a shadow of its limitless possibilities. Your power lies in putting your best self forward each day.

It took some time before I saw the results I desired in my life; it was not an overnight success. I was willing to go through the process no matter how long it was going to take. That being said, I want you to be fully aware that it is going to take time and **you must be committed to the process**. Success does not happen overnight, but it can happen for any woman who is willing to make focused plans; be committed to the process and never give up. That which you offer authentically of yourself returns to you in life and career success.

Who decides whether you will be successful or not? (Cue the "Jeopardy" theme music.) The final answer…….**You do**! In order to prosper and succeed, you must first have the desire to do so and be willing to stay the course. You are the Queen of your results. Women who feel in control of life can withstand an enormous amount of change and thrive on it.

On this journey, I will be your coach; you may not like everything I ask you to do, but you will appreciate it later when you see the results. If you are going to have a life changing experience, you must participate in the process.

I promise you, I will give you the principles and strategies, and the only requirement I have as your coach is that you take full responsibility for the results and be committed to the process.

The first step in changing your life is to decide to take responsibility for having what you want. If you are not satisfied with your current condition, rewrite your goals by taking action and doing something different. You are in charge of your life, so decide how you want it to look and then make it look that way. Women who allow things to control them are being reactive, not proactive. **Proactive women take control and do whatever is necessary to accomplish their goals.**

When I started on the journey of success, I had to get my stinking thinking out the way so a new way of thinking could be developed. It took time to develop this new prosperous way of thinking because I had some deep rooted erroneous beliefs I had to get rid of. I played the victim game and blamed everyone under the sun for the unfavorable circumstances in my life. I blamed my parents, I blamed the school system, I blamed the government, and I even blamed my siblings. It is difficult to feel good about yourself when you give your power away by making something or someone else responsible for your life.

Most women fail to reach their personal goals because they're in the dark about what's influencing their behavior. To get what I desired in life, I had to go through a total transformation, a complete change in my mind about some of the things I believed to be true; and honestly, it was quite a struggle. When you have been raised with beliefs that have been passed down for generations, then wake up one day and learn that some of those beliefs have been keeping you back, it is a fight to change. Change is difficult when you are not willing to give up a counter-productive belief. So, if you must change, why resist it?

The problem is that to grow, to take the journeys on which our growth is predicated, we must confront our own immaturity, selfishness and lack of courage. Changing your thinking is the most important thing you can do to change the results of your actions. The key to making significant changes in life is to make little changes; it is a process. To make real changes in our life, we first must be prepared to take responsibility for ourselves and our choices. Don't wait for "someone" to fix things in your life. **Create the change YOU want to see.**

All true success is personally defined. You decide the goal, the pace and the parameters around which you are willing to be successful. You have only you to please in your success. You create your world by the way you think. If you are willing to change your thinking, you can change your feelings. If you change your feelings, you can change your actions. And changing your actions - based on good thinking - can change your life.

Where your mind goes, creative energy flows. In order for you to become prosperous, you must think in a different order of magnitude from those who are content with just getting by. One of the reasons some women don't achieve their dreams is that they desire to change their results without changing their thinking.

There are no limits to attaining your most desired hopes and desires as long as you can define what it is you want to achieve in life. A great deal of what you have perceived as limits in your life are actually limits you have placed upon yourself. The good news is that you have already begun to eliminate them. You began the moment you picked up this book. This book will help you address them directly.

It is a mistake to assume that all women want and need the same thing; what motivates one person may not move another person at all. It is easier to understand yourself if you know what motivates you. Someone once said to me and I still reflect on this insight constantly: **"Do not die with your music left inside of you; be all that God created you to be. Be more, do more and have more."**

I realized God created me in His image and wealth was the will of God for me. God did not predetermine who would be prosperous or who would live in lack. He simply created His spiritual laws and freely gave them to everyone. Every women then has a choice to implement the laws of prosperity or the laws of scarcity.

I had what you would call an awakening, the day of reckoning. I was not going to accept the lifestyle "I" created with my thoughts and actions. This was the day I took back my power and accepted responsibility for the mess I created. I became aware of who I was, who I belonged to, and what was promised to me. I realized that the life each of us live is the life within the limits of our own thinking.

> "The greatest failure is to not try. Once you find something you love to do, be the best at doing it. Faith creates; doubt destroys. Faith opens the door to all things desirable in life; doubt closes it." Deborah Francis

I sought out the truth about wealth and its availability to me. It was always there for my enjoyment but I could not recognize it. It is like when you hear someone say, "I will be happy when..." I realized that it was not the stuff that was going to make me happy, it was the freedom from scarcity. When I say freedom from scarcity, I am not just speaking in terms of finances; I am talking about a form of thinking. Scarcity is a mindset that creates unfavorable circumstances in all areas of your life. **Every woman who has really prospered or reached an exceptional level of success has one thing in common: they have broken the bondage of their limitations**.

It was when I took an honest look at my life and the results I was getting that I came to a moment of truth: I was not happy with the results; I wanted more. I desired to have meaningful relationships. I desired a healthy body—a body that when I looked in the mirror, I smiled and said, "You look good." I desired the finances to be able to provide for my family and be a blessing to others. I understood that I had to expand my prosperity consciousness in order to break out of a scarcity mentality.

I could either take responsibility or play the victim game. I realized that if I take the position of victim, I lose power. If I choose responsibility, then I have the power to do something about the circumstances in my life. The more responsibility I accepted for the consequences of my actions, the more power I assumed. I began to change my thinking, my belief and my environment. I learned how to let go of negative people, places and things that did not add value to my life. My character and future began to be molded by my thoughts, actions and associations.

Prosperity began to demonstrate itself in my life in many ways, and I am truly grateful. It started out with gaining an understanding of my relationship with GOD. I am not here to convert you to any religious belief, because that is a personal journey. I just applied the spiritual teachings that I received and I got results in my life. I learned to accept me and love myself and others. I am blessed with a wonderful family who loves me for me. I have wonderful relationships all across the country. On the business side, I doubled my income for the past 10 years.

I have used the principles in this book to achieve more than I ever dreamed, imagined or ever desired. I have found what is truly important in life and I am in awe of the unlimited possibilities that still lie ahead. This is not just for me or a select few; the same is going to happen for you as you apply these principles. My desire is for you to develop a success consciousness that cannot be taken away. You deserve to be successful. It is not for a chosen few; it is for everyone who desires it and applies the correct principles.

I truly believe God showed me the way so that I can teach other women the principles of success. There is a pattern in everything. We just need the right lens to see it. Through our attitudes, we either limit ourselves and stay stuck where we are-or we give ourselves permission to change and move ahead.

You were created in God's image so everything you need, you already have. The tools within you must be cultivated and applied properly to achieve the life you desire. You have to face your fears. The best way to do this is to confront them directly.

If it is change that you seek, like having loving and fun relationships or control over your life, you must break free from all self-destructive habits, conditioning and thinking, and then adopt a complete surrender to prosperous thinking. You have the power within to change anything about yourself. Everything that happens in your life begins with making a decision.

There will come an important moment in your life when you discover for yourself the great mystery of life: things may happen to you, and things may happen around you, but the only thing that really matters are the things that happen in you.

As we embark on this journey, the question you must ask yourself is "What do I want out of life?" Many women live their lives without ever asking this important question. As a result, their life becomes a series of events dictated by external circumstances instead of inner needs and desires. Unless you know what your desires are, you have no choice but to bounce from one activity to another, looking for a quick fix and forced to accept whatever comes your way.

This book is meant to challenge you into actively pursuing a new level of wealth consciousness by understanding and applying these principles in your life. You will not grasp the message in this book unless you read and apply it with an open mind. Wealth is everywhere; become aware of endless opportunities that surround you. **You Are Built To Prosper!**

The Miracle Is You

Miracles! Miracles! Have you not looked at yourself lately?

The Miracle Is You

Have you not seen your gifts and talents that even surprise you?

You are a miracle designed, so others may see the glory of God.

Miracles! Miracles!
Go take a look in a mirror and see the image of God.

Oh! Yeah! That miracle.
It's You

By: Blossom V. Brackman

THE FOUNDATION

> "If your fear of being judged is keeping you from implementing ideas that may change your life, what else is that fear holding you back from? Those that take action in spite of fear accomplish great things, while those chained to fear are shouting "that's impossible" **Deborah Francis**

One of the requirements in reading and understanding a map is that you have to know exactly where you are before you can figure out where you are going. And that is exactly what we have purposed to do in this book. We want to help you find your authentic self. Internal and external challenges will test your search for authenticity. You cannot be a quitter on this journey; you have to consistently learn, do and review. Successful women are characterized by this attitude of positive self-expectancy. They expect to succeed more often than they fail. They expect to win more often than they lose.

Are you ready for change? Are you willing to develop yourself until you break free from the bondage of defeat? It is going to take effort on your part, and we are going to do our part. We are going to provide you with all the tools you need to help you become all that you desire, but it is up to you to pick the tools up and use them.

Few women are aware of the true meaning of life, of what is really worthwhile and what it is to know oneself. Only those who know themselves can succeed. Your life means something; you may not have found that meaning yet, but you will. For you to be prosperous, you will have to deliberately choose to be. Choice is the means and the end.

Your prosperity will come from your choices in the way you use your mind. You have a reason to prosper; you have a purpose beyond what you think. You were not put on this earth to live an average life and just get by; you are to live life to the maximum.

You must give yourself permission to be prosperous. You were created to expand; it is natural. Wanting is how you grow. You are not selfish or greedy when you desire the best for your life; you are stretching to realize your greatest potential. Many people are not willing to do what is necessary to reach their fullest potential and that is why they will go to their graves with regrets. Many women push their dreams and purpose aside for a paycheck or they make excuses about not having enough time to do what they know in their heart is the right thing to do.

I remember the time when I broke my ankle in my senior year of college. I had four months left until it was time to graduate. Everyone made it seem like it would be too much for me to get to all my classes on crutches in the snowy hills of upstate New York. I was determined to finish and complete my degree on time. After much prayer, I was clear that no matter what, or how difficult others thought it was going to be, I was going to succeed. When I discussed with my mother that I was planning to return to college which was over seven hours away, she was very concerned. She turned away for a moment looked up and said, "If you plan to finish and graduate on time, I am going to be there with you to help. I will be your extra legs." My mother took a bus every other week to my college and stayed with me for up to four days, helping me with getting up and down stairs in sometimes what was up to five inches of ice and snow.

Two weeks into this routine, my aunt (who is like a second mother to me) said that the weeks that my mother was unable to travel up to my college, she was going to make herself available to come and help me. This was women working together at its finest. My goal was to graduate despite all odds. There was one terribly cold and icy day that I was leaving class and I was determined to make it down some icy stairs on my own. I slipped to my dismay and I was trembling because I thought that I had fractured my ankle again that was still in a cast. On my back I looked up and began to cry. I asked myself, "Is this really all worth it?" At that moment, my professor, who was like a mentor to me, saw me on back crying and struggling to get up and asked if she could help me. I took her arm and was brought to my feet on what seemed like an ice skating ring. I looked my professor in her eyes and told her, "Thank you." Then I said, "I am going to do whatever it takes, because God has continued to put women in my path who wanted me to succeed and who believed in me."

Life is about more understanding, more wisdom, more love, more laughter, more rain, more sunshine, more giving, more receiving. **We are to be a blessing to others while we are here, and the only way to be a blessing is to be blessed ourselves. It is only right that you live a life of success and victory**. Your external world of your health, relationships and financial accomplishment will be a mirror image of your inner world of preparation. The only part of the equation that you can control is your conscious thoughts; and if you can keep your conscious thoughts on what you want, eventually your external world of reality and experiences will reflect it back to you.

Rather than allowing others to define success for you, take the time today to create your own definition. Have the courage to measure your success by standards that are meaningful for your life. How do you define success? What does success look like to you? Take a few moments and think about these questions. Only you can answer these questions; success is personal.

Many women may tend to equate success with money and material wealth. Even though these things can be an outward sign of your own career or business success or that of your family, it reflects only a small piece of the bigger picture that is your life. The principles described in this book are about you becoming all that God designed you to be. There must be a conscious effort on your part to learn the necessary principles and obtain what you need to be prosperous. I know you are on the right track; you invested in yourself by purchasing this book and once again, I commend you. **You are a student of the game of life**.

You are going to learn how to live and work from the inside. When you live from the inside, the outside circumstances have to fall into place. There is nothing in this world that can stop you but you. Knowing and applying the principles of success will set you free from the bondage of lack, want and defeat. To perform at your best, you need to know who you are and why you think and feel the way you do. It is only when you understand and accept yourself that you can begin moving forward in other areas of your life. A successful life should encompass far more than your work or finances, although they are a part of the big picture. A fulfilling life in all areas is a successful life.

> "You are the writer of your life story, you are the director of your life movie." Rhonda Byrne

Life is what you make it, so why not make your life a prosperous one? We live in an ever-increasing universe filled with abundance. We were created by God, who is available to fulfill our every need and desire. It is our divine nature to want more and to gravitate towards abundance. Every woman naturally wants to be provided for, to be and have all that she is capable of being and having. We were created to manifest good on this earth.

On some level, every woman wants a life filled with an abundance of love, joy, happiness, health, wonderful relationships, peace, and we cannot forget money. It is natural to want the best for you and your family, the best foods for your body which is your temple, the best clothing, and the most comfortable home filled with all the amenities you desire. Living prosperously is godly; you become blessed to be a blessing to others. Opportunities and blessings come to the woman who embraces a prosperous attitude. Other women have created the life of their dreams; so can you.

Creating a prosperous life comes with a price and only those who are willing to pay the price will become prosperous. You may be thinking, "What price must I pay?" You have to change the old negative images and habits of how you think, talk, and feel about wealth. **You must claim your birthright—the rich life**. Will it be an easy task? Absolutely not! Some so-called "gurus" may tell you that you can quantum leap to success but my friend, it just does not work that way. It requires work and 90 percent of the work is on your thinking, beliefs, and attitude.

Many women today give up because they are not committed to the process of developing themselves. Due to their lack of commitment, they settle for what life gives them. But you, my friend, I desire the best for you and you will receive it only if you believe and stay committed to the process. We are apt to think of women who have been successful in life and in business as being greatly favored by fortune, and we account for it in all sorts of ways except the right one. The truth is that their success represents their expectation of themselves, the sum of their creative and habitual thinking. They have created what they have and what they are out of their constructive thought and their unquenchable faith in The Higher Power and themselves.

We must not only believe that we can succeed, but we must believe with all our heart. Our life manifests from our most dominant thoughts and feelings. Just as whatever we plant grows, that which we focus our attention on multiplies. **You are the fruit of the thoughts you have planted and nourished.** If you want a better harvest, you must plant better thoughts. Whatever we put in our mind comes out in our lives.

We select the circumstances that occur in our lives by choosing how and where we focus our attention. Every negative thought has a consequence. If you want success, then you must have successful thoughts and a positive conviction that you will attain success.

> "We are taught you must blame your father, your sisters, your brothers, the school, and the teachers-but never blame yourself. It's never your fault. But it's always your fault, because if you wanted to change you're the one who has got to change."
> Katharine Hepburn

Many women are unaware of the abundance that is available to them, some believe they do not deserve to have wealth, and then there are those who may believe that to deny oneself of wealth is noble. There is nothing noble about living in lack, not knowing how you are going to pay the bills or feed your family. Go tell a woman who is trying to feed her family that it is noble for her children to be hungry. Make sure you run after you make that statement.

I believe some women use the denial factor as an excuse to not use their God-given ability. Who wants to be a person who pays their bills late, receives handouts from others, or is always owing and not owning? The individual who persists in holding their mental attitude towards scarcity, or who is always thinking of their hard luck and failure to succeed, can by no possibility go in the opposite direction where the goal of prosperity resides.

Are you hoping for greater health, wealth, love, and success? The time is now; the harvest has come. You shall reap the abundance you desire if you have faith and believe that there is more than enough. There is a time when the possible and the prosperous spirit in you are going to meet and manifest your desires. You should always desire that which is good for you and your family. To seek a better life, you first have to decide what you want for your life. If you learn to take responsibility for your life, you will come to an understanding that you are where you are today because of the decisions you have made. A decision that you can make today is that you will do what it takes to develop a prosperous mindset.

Simply wishing for a better life is insufficient. If you are to make any steps toward your definite objectives, then you need to have a determined attitude, bordering on obsession, to fulfill that desire. It does not matter what you desire. It may be a desire to be a better person in your relationships, or it could be to take better care of your health. As soon as you empower yourself to prosper and overcome any fears of failure, or even success, you will realize that you deserve all that you desire and move towards what you want rather than towards what you do not want. You will be consciously making the decision to win in life.

Think big about life; have faith that whatever you desire will come to pass if you remain persistent and consistent in acting on your vision. This is not one of those books where you are filled with affirmations and then expect abundance to fall in your lap while you are sitting at home watching the television. There is nothing wrong with declaring affirmations, but some action must be taken afterwards. Why is it that people in our society lead lives of quiet desperation? Less than 10%, and I am being modest, achieve real success in life. We live in a world that provides the most opportunity to be prosperous and live a life of fulfillment.

In today's society, many expect the worst; if you need proof, take me up on this challenge. When you get in your office on Monday morning, go to the nearest water cooler, coffee maker or even get in the elevator with someone and you will hear so much negative talk that it could literally drive you insane. Many are concerned about their job, what people think about them, how they look, and are constantly complaining about their spouse with people who do not need to know their personal business.

These people are energy drainers. They bring rain to the picnic. Most people are comfortable with negativity, and you can never make changes when you are comfortable. A wise mentor once told me: "Success is outside of your comfort zone."

> "When you focus on the little things, you lose sight of your vision. An obstacle is something you see, when you take your eyes off the goal. Focus is a discipline." Deborah Francis

Some women tend to sabotage themselves when they are conflicted about their goals or feel unworthy of success. **How do you determine your self-worth?** By money, good looks, education, fine clothes, an executive office, or a luxury automobile? When a woman has a low self-image, she sometimes tries to compensate for these feelings by trying to increase her value through the attainment of material things or by condemning those who have achieved success. The key is learn to love yourself. As simple as this may seem, it is very difficult for women who are used to self-criticism and self-sabotage.

In developing your foundation of being prosperous, you must develop a strong sense of self-worth without the attachment to material things. To be truly happy, you need a clear sense of direction. You need to feel that your life stands for something, that you are somehow making a valuable contribution to your world. **There is nothing wrong with having expensive things in life. I enjoy opulence, but my self-worth is not tied to my accumulation of material wealth**. My true wealth is the inner me and no one can take that away. I do not need permission or validation from anybody to be wealthy.

Wealth comes from the inside; no one can give it to you. Just as I cannot give you a body that is fit, because I cannot go into the gym and do all the cardio exercises for you. It is all up to you; that is your responsibility. **I know many may desire a quick fix to increase their prosperity, but developing wealth is an inner process**. Expressing your uniqueness is what makes you successful. There is not another woman who can do exactly what you can do, because no other woman has your same life experiences mixed with your unique strengths. Consciously developing and using your own natural gifts and talents can make you stand out and be successful. Learn to feel deserving of all life has to offer by loving and nurturing yourself.

Women and Money

What were you told about money when you were a child? We have grown up in a society which dictates that men are supposed to be the bread-winners in all areas dealing with money and financial success. A "glass ceiling" has been created and some have personally felt the repercussions. But there are plenty of women who have shattered this so-called glass ceiling. Many women have gone on to build successful businesses and careers that generate high incomes for them. For some women, earning money is not just about economic power—it is about having more choices, freedom, and taking control of their life. Women must advocate for themselves. Nobody else will do it for them.

Money is a tool and a resource. Someone once said to me, "Money is not everything." My reply was, "Go tell your mortgage and credit card company that." Many people make having money a morality statement when it is neither moral nor immoral. Money itself is neither good nor evil. It has the ability to do only what its owner wants it to do. The owner is in charge. If you need proof, place a $100 bill on the table and see if it jumps up and does some evil. Waiting…. Waiting… Nothing yet? In all my years on this earth, Benjamin Franklin never forced me into doing something outside of my will. **Money has no power in itself, but having control over how it will be used gives you power. Money serves its possessor without question; it is ready to be used for good or evil at its owner's discretion.**

By changing your ingrained reactions and beliefs, you can achieve new, positive results. Begin to view money as any other tool you have available for your use. How you use that tool will determine whether or not it does harm or good. Cars, ink, paper, hammer, nails, gasoline, airplanes, money—all these can improve the quality of a person's life. However, all of them can cause severe harm when misused. You may be asking, "How can ink and paper cause severe harm if misused?" Have you written or read a story about someone who was degraded or had a claim against their character? This demonstrates an example where the pen is mightier than the sword.

The blessing or harm to your life is determined by whether or not these tools are wisely operated under your control. Just as with money, you are in danger when it begins to rule you instead of you ruling it. If you are staying up all night tossing and turning thinking about getting money to pay your bills, then money and bills just became your master. Here is my recommendation drink some hot chocolate and go to sleep.

Money is meant to be used with a strong sense of discernment and wisdom. In order to handle large amounts of money, you must be mentally prepared to handle it. Money will control you if you do not have the right mindset for it.

Studies show that no more than five women out of a hundred who have made money know what to do with it and are able to hold on to it. If you need further proof, study the people who have won the lottery. Most of the winners end up worse off than before they gained their winnings. Why? They were not mentally prepared for the riches they've received. They gained a large amount of money but they had the wrong money mindset (easy come, easy go). They never developed the proper philosophy of saving and investing their money; they had the hand-to-mouth mentality.

There's never been a better time for women to map out their financial futures. Achieving financial freedom is one of the most important goals and responsibilities of your life. A feeling of freedom is essential to the achievement of any other important goal, and you cannot be free until and unless you have enough money so that you are no longer preoccupied with it. When you decide exactly what you want and what your financial picture will look like, you will be able to achieve your goals faster than you might have imagined possible.

If you want the same results as wealthy people, then you must take the necessary action to create those results. Wealth is an equal opportunist. When you unite your passion with your God-given ability, money will flow to you like streams leading to an ocean. The women who succeed in life commit to doing what they love and the money follows.

It is important to learn how to master money rather than be enslaved by it. Money is a good tool if used properly. Every decision you make with your money is an investment. To have control over your money and to become the master of money, you must develop a wealthy mindset. Your thoughts, feelings and attitude about money will influence the outcome of your finances. Wealth is a matter of expectation. Whatever personal definition you have for wealth, it is essential to understand that wealth is not an accident. It is absolutely predictable and can be earned by anyone.

The truth is that wealth is no respecter of persons. **Wealth begins on the inside of you; it is a state of mind**. Wealth is not due to luck or circumstances or environment. You have the power to create wealth for yourself. This power was given to you.

If you have not used your power up to this point, then you have no one to blame but yourself. Take responsibility for your life. Your mindset created the life you currently live and if it is not the life you desire, then you and you alone have the power to change it. You need to change your life philosophy if the one you have now is not working for you. For most people, their main concern is, "Can I pay my bills?" Life is so much bigger than bills; if you want to change your position in life, you will have to expand your perspective.

> "If you don't go after what you want, you'll never have it. If you don't ask, the answer is always no. If you don't step forward, you're always in the same place." Nora Roberts

It does not matter where you are spiritually, physically, relationally, or financially today; there is hope. Have confidence in your ability to create the life you truly desire. Being confident is entirely a matter of mind. Without confidence in your own uniqueness, in your God-given abilities, you cannot succeed at living a prosperous life. But with self-confidence, you can succeed at whatever you choose. So why do we have a large amount of women who are not living a prosperous life if all it takes is believing in themselves? It is because a large percentage of women make themselves unhappy by feeling they are not good enough. It may be a fact that you are not tall or able to wear designer clothes or drive a luxury automobile, but you can still become confident. It is attitude that counts. This is not theory.

When I first met my husband, I was a school teacher and I had a master's degree in secondary education. He had an hourly paying job and was pursuing his college degree. For the first couple of years of our relationship, I made more income than my husband. I knew on my own I was destined for greatness but as the scripture says in Matthew 18:19: Again, I tell you that if two of you on earth agree about anything you ask for, it will be done for you by my Father in heaven. I knew together we would be wealthy. I never judged my husband by how much he made; my attitude was that he had the potential to become multi-millionaire. I was impressed with his confidence and his vision about being an entrepreneur; it was one of the qualities that won me over.

Years later we have created multiple streams of income. What I truly admire about my husband is that he always encouraged me to be independent financially. He always expressed that if something was to happen to him, he wanted me to be able to live without depending on anyone else.

Desire is a force that sets things in motion to bring about its own fulfillment. Thus, to begin fulfilling your desires, you must first do something constructive. There is nothing half-hearted about true desire; it is intense and powerful. If properly developed and expressed, a strong desire can produce great wealth in your life. Only those who become "wealth conscious" ever accumulate wealth.

Wealth consciousness means that the mind has become so thoroughly saturated with the desire for wealth, that one can see oneself already in possession of it. **Wealth is about creating a life of great health, loving relationships, doing what you love, and also having money to provide for your needs and to be a help to others.**

The Bible states in Deuteronomy 8:18: **"But thou shalt remember the LORD thy God: for it is he that giveth thee power to get wealth, that he may establish his covenant which he sware unto thy fathers, as it is this day."** God would not give you the power to get wealth if He did not intend for you to use that power and become wealthy! The decision to live in prosperity is yours. God did His part, now you must do yours by making a life-changing decision today to accept your God-given rights to live abundantly and reject the destructive laws of scarcity.

If you have a positive mental attitude toward wealth and you have vigorous faith, you are going to demonstrate wealth in your life. Your attitude is a composite of your thoughts, feelings and actions. The only way you can improve the results you are getting in life is to take full responsibility for your attitude. Only then will you be able to improve your results. **Continue to strive intelligently and persistently to realize your vision**. This is the law of prosperity; if you obey the law, you will get the results. The law does not discriminate. Prosperity is not an accident. It is time to reflect on where you are presently and where you want to be in regards to your life.

I would like for you to take a few moments and write in great detail your answer to the following question: What do you really want out of life?

What are your personal strengths? Write the qualities you like best about yourself.

_____
_____
_____
_____
_____
_____
_____
_____
_____
_____
_____
_____
_____
_____
_____
_____
_____
_____
_____
_____
_____
_____
_____
_____
_____

What areas of your life need development?

Who would you like to become? Strive to visualize who you want to be in regards to living a life based on your passion.

How do you define wealth, prosperity, and riches?

Are you motivated to achieve what you really want in life?

STOP: Did you complete the exercises? Are you just reading to say you know or are you working for full understanding? I desire the best for you, so if you have not done the exercises and you refuse to participate, put this book down; this book is not for the fainthearted. I want results in your life, so please complete all exercises. **Remember, this is your personal journey.** Transformation is never effortless; nothing changes unless we do. If you completed the exercises, I applaud your commitment. The reason you must complete the exercises listed is because every time you write your vision or goals, you begin to program your desires deeper into your subconscious mind, which can either work for you or against you.

To prosper means you have become prosperous in your mindset. What a person is, not what they have, is the measure of real prosperity. Having an abundant mentality affects all areas of your life, not just your bank account. We need a new perspective in redefining what true prosperity and success are, which is the result of having developed a consciousness of prosperity, realizing that we all have the necessary tools we need to create our prosperity.

It does not matter what you have achieved or how much cash flow you have coming in; if you live with an attitude of scarcity and limitation, or if you expect for someone or something to fulfill you, you are not going to be satisfied.

When you have a prosperity consciousness, you will have peace of mind and an abundance of wealth, health, and wonderful, loving relationships in life.

You are in charge of your own destiny. All that you need or want is here for the asking; believe it and accept it. God's will is to do some powerful and amazing things in your life, and He is ready when you are. Are you tired of living an ordinary life? Wealth is a choice, not a chance. When you really desire to live a life of wealth and abundance, you will.

You become mentally rich when you think rich thoughts. You become emotionally rich when you have rich feelings towards yourself and others. You become spiritually rich when you discover the true riches of the Kingdom within. If you could see a picture of the mental processes of whatever is held in the mind, attracting the things and circumstances that correspond to your thoughts, and if you could see the heartaches, the failures, bad health, bad business deals, the debt starting towards you because you have attracted these things in your thoughts, then you would stop worrying and complaining about the things you do not want and start focusing on the things you do want. This results in attracting more abundance instead of lack, success instead of failure.

There is a shocking truth about wealth: it adores a person who has a healthy attitude towards it. Thoughts of your mind have made you what you are, and the thoughts of your mind will make you whatever you become from this day forward. Once you realize this, you will come to a full understanding that people, places, conditions, and events cannot keep wealth from coming to you. This is the power of prosperous thinking.

> "We would rather build value and earn what we are worth, than eat crumbs and accept less than what we are worth."
> Deborah Francis

When you are prosperous, it has a huge impact on your life and it gives you options. It gives you the ability to provide some memorable experiences with your family. It also affects the quality of your relationships, what you eat, the people you can help, what you drive, and where you vacation; this earth has some beautiful places you would love to experience.

We all have the right to be prosperous. Meditate on those powerful words for a minute and let them become a part of you. We get what we believe we deserve. No more, no less.

Do you believe you deserve to have more than enough?

We don't allow ourselves to have what we want until we believe – truly believe – that we deserve it. What you believe you deserve are self-imposed limits that reflect your unconscious and conscious feelings of worth. Many women become uncomfortable when they get close to personal success and then they become self-destructive. Part of the answer seems to be in how they have defined prosperity and how they may have been programmed with negative thoughts toward prosperity. This programming may have come from their family, the environment they grew up in, or their own limiting beliefs.

To get rid of all the old destructive and erroneous beliefs and develop a true prosperity consciousness requires a total transformation on the inside. You must let go of any old negative concepts of yourself as being inadequate, unsure, or unworthy, or any belief that will stand in the way of you creating the life you desire.

> "We are all here for some special reason. Stop being a prisoner of your past. Become the architect of your future." Robin Sharma

You have the ability to be prosperous, but prosperity begins to come once you decide to prosper. It is a choice; it is a decision. Through proper planning and consistent action, you can develop a prosperity consciousness that will lead you to wealth as well as increased abundance in all phases of your life. It is wonderful when you come to the full understanding that you have the power to create a life of your choice and you are able to get what you really want and not just what is handed to you.

The power is ours. To increase our prosperity, we must start with what we have, and we have plenty. Our problem is not with the seed, but with the soil. Seeds are being sown (wealth ideas) all the time, but the soil (mind) in which it is being sown is not right, so the seed cannot flourish. Prepare the soil (mind) and the seed will produce a harvest"......If YOU understand this, it will change your life

Imagine living your life with the sensation of being fully satisfied and yet being open to the world. When we understand and apply the principles of prosperity, we know we can handle any turn of events that might take place. We have what it takes to live freely without worry and fear. There is no one thing that needs to happen and no obstacles to get by to start feeling prosperous. We do not need to wait until we have enough of anything in order to be happy. If it is true that we attract only what we are, then let us be all that we can be now.

Let us think for a moment: say there are two doors in front of you. The first door once opened, leads to a life of abundance, wealth, prosperity, joy, peace and happiness. And the second door once opened, leads to a life filled with desperation, pain, lack, fear and a constant state of wanting. You hold the key that can open either door; you choose which door you will open. **It is your choice**. It is up to you.

> "You walk in the direction in which you face; if you persist in facing challenges and setbacks in your life, you cannot expect to reach a solution. The magnet must be true to itself, it must attract things like itself" Deborah Francis

Keep reminding yourself that you have all the power within you that is greater than any current condition or circumstance you may be facing. **Now let's continue our journey!**

CHAPTER I
I AM WHAT I THINK I AM

CHAPTER I
I AM WHAT I THINK I AM

> "I am so beautiful, sometimes people weep when they see me. And it has nothing to do with what I look like really, it is just that I gave myself the power to say that I am beautiful, and if I could do that, maybe there is hope for them too. And the great divide between the beautiful and the ugly will cease to be. Because we are all what we choose." Margaret Cho

We are born with the power to create through our thoughts. Our lives are designed by our thoughts; everything originates in our thinking. Each of us is a living magnet. Our thoughts are energy, and we attract into our lives the people and circumstances that harmonize with our most dominant thoughts. Our thought energy has the power to develop from the world of ideas to the world of reality.

Our life at this present moment is the representation of our thought patterns. Our greatest and most priceless possession is our mind. Our mind is creative and if we desire to attract different people, circumstances and events, we have to change what is going on in our minds and thought patterns.

God has given us a powerful and creative tool: "the mind." Wealth begins in the mind. We receive this power to create from our ability to use our imagination. Everything that has been created by someone was first an imaginative idea of the mind. We are surrounded by creative ideas that have manifested into the physical reality. Our mind is a spiritual estate. The results we receive in life and in our businesses are shaped by our dominate thoughts, our beliefs, and our attitude.

> "The women that have the courage to do the things, they were told they cannot do, are the ones who succeed. Stepping outside of your comfort zone is not always easy." Deborah Francis

We can change our circumstances by changing the way we think and feel, what we believe and say to ourselves, and the actions we take. However, the secret of prosperity is that it begins within your own thoughts and feelings. There is a powerful magnet within you that attracts to you what you are.

I have noticed that people who may have had some sort of destructive relationship in their life continue to attract those same types of people. Hurt people attract hurt people, abundance attracts abundance, and lack attracts lack. This was a wake-up call for me once I realized I was focusing more on what I did not want and not on what I desired.

I used to literally spend hours of the day focusing on how I was going to pay my bills. I gave those bills a lot of power, putting so much worry into not having enough to pay them. I was acting like the bill collectors were the boogie monster coming to eat me. Thinking about them continually created a feeling of fear, and then I began to talk in fear and act in fear. My thoughts became energy that manifested itself into a late bill. We attract everything that happens in our life. The negative experiences scream for attention, but you have to embrace the positive ones.

> "The more you praise and celebrate your life, the more there is in life to celebrate." Oprah Winfrey

Once we focus our thoughts on things that we desire, and feel as though they are so, we give energy to our desires to manifest itself in our lives. It is imperative that we think in line with our divine inheritance, which is prosperity.

Whatever your mind is taught to expect, it will build, produce, and bring forth for you. A scarcity mentality is the opposite of the prosperity mentality. Women who function under a scarcity mentality believe that there is never enough in life—never enough love, money, or opportunities. When you function under this mentality of "never enough," you restrict your creative ability to produce, and you begin to act in haste because you believe that someone else is going to get what you desire. Our expectations affect our results.

What are your expectations about life? Do you feel you have a purpose in life? Describe what you want to contribute to the world.

The reason why most people are unhappy is that they are living under the expectation and programming of others.

Most of our programming has been influenced by negative thoughts—not only our own thoughts, but all of those around us. Our parents, our friends and even the television can program us with the wrong expectations of life. It is a cycle that must be broken. The Apostle Paul wrote in Romans 12:2: **"And be not conformed to this world: but be ye transformed by the renewing of your mind, that ye may prove what is that good, and acceptable, and perfect, will of God."**

It is important that in everything you do in life, you set your own expectations. Always expect the best from yourself and always expect to continue to get better; you are doing that now, and that is why you are reading this book.

Whatever we expect with conviction becomes our own self-fulfilling prophecy. Through their thoughts, most people are often attracting things to themselves that they do not consciously desire. Your thoughts are creative not because you wish, hope, pray, or long for it to be so, they are creative because there is a creative law operating upon it. You are where and what you are because of the dominating thoughts in your mind.

> **"If you realized how powerful YOU are, you would make a conscious effort to not think negative thoughts." Deborah Francis**

Think big because you are big. Think generously because you are made to express generosity. There are no limits except the limits you place on your own imagination. Stop chasing after lack; instead, come to the full understanding that wealth was custom made just for you. It is certain that you cannot believe in wealth, prosperity, and abundance if you identify yourself as an individual of lack. Forget lack and think only of wealth in all areas of your life.

You have absolute control over one thing and that is your thoughts. You cannot control the weather or your kids, spouse, or anything for that matter outside of your own beliefs, thoughts, attitudes and actions. **You are the key that will unlock the door to your desires**. So concentrate on what you do have control over; your thoughts. And that can be the most powerful control of all. Prosperity belongs to you, and it will only come to you if you affirm its presence in your thoughts.

Your mind must create the good you desire, for then and only then will you experience the good you have created. **You can produce definite results only when your mind has been given definite desires**. The law of attraction says that you are a living magnet. It says that your thoughts create a force field of energy that radiates out from you and attracts back into your life people and circumstances in harmony with them.

Any thought you have, combined with an emotion, positive or negative, radiates out from you and attracts back into your life the people, circumstances, ideas, and opportunities consistent with it. If there is failure and lack in your life, it is because you first imagined it in your mind.

> **"The minute you settle for less than you deserve, you get even less than you settled for." Maureen Dowd**

We have the power to change, to be what we want to be, and to have what we want to have. That power is thought. When our thoughts are repeated often enough, they form a pattern. These thought patterns actually program our mind. Whatever we are programming our mind to create, it creates. Successful women think about what they want, and how to get it, most of the time. When you think and talk about what you want and how to get it, you feel happier and in greater control of your life.

We all desire to have the best and to live a full and complete life. Some women have a hard time accepting that life is not all about struggling and that it is completely fine to live a life of abundance. I do not believe that nor have the desire to understand that type of thinking.

We all have been given the necessary tools and power to create the life we desire. Some women need to enlarge their vision of what they want to do in their life and come to a full understanding of prosperity. As long as your mind is working, you can do extraordinary things.

Your thoughts and your willingness to take action are the only attributes that stand in your way of attaining what you want in life. You can have what you think you deserve and what you believe you can have. If you are convinced you should not have or are unworthy of getting what you want, you will unconsciously create an environment that will prevent you from becoming successful.

Unsuccessful people think and talk about things they do not want. They think and talk about their problems and pain and the people they do not like. Sometimes, their whole life revolves around their complaints and criticism; and the more they think and complain about what they do not want, the unhappier they become. My mentor shared some insight with me a couple of years ago: "Small people talk about people, average people talk about events, and wealthy people talk about ideas."

Learn to think abundantly. Think of the vastness of everything like the limitless of space, or the grains of sand on the seashore which cannot be counted. Think how abundant, how lavish, how rich nature is. Develop a habit of seeing abundance in everything in order to multiply the good you already possess. Be conscious of the law of abundance. As you develop a consciousness of prosperity, you will experience improvements in life.

> "Don't limit yourself. Many people limit themselves to what they think they can do. You can go as far as your mind lets you. What you believe, remember, you can achieve." Mary Kay Ash

It is important that you maintain a strict censorship over your thinking. Just as a gardener watches over their garden to protect it from weeds and anything that can destroy its beauty, so you must refuse entrance to any thoughts you do not wish to see manifested in your life. What you accept completely in your mind, you will get in experience regardless of conditions or circumstances. So what is keeping you from believing in yourself and achieving your goals? Your self-limiting thoughts... and you can conquer those.

Guard your mind at all costs; it is the garden of your soul. It is in the garden of your mind where your hopes, dreams, and desires are blossoming into fulfillment. If you allow the weeds of fear, doubt, and hatred to grow in the garden of your mind, it will choke out the beauty of hope until despair alone remains. The way to eliminate the self-doubt that holds many prisoners is by filling your mind with faith in God, who created you in His image; this will give you a powerful, realistic faith in yourself. Reprogram your mind to be confident instead of self-critical. **Make positive expectations the default of your thinking. Turn your mind into a prosperous-thinking, power-producing machine**. Plant in the garden of your mind seeds of love, joy, wealth, abundance, peace, gratitude, and happiness.

Exercise: Turn off the television and take the battery out the phone (I know, taking the battery out is a little extreme but peace and quiet comes at a cost). Set aside at least 20 minutes a day to clear your mind. Find a quiet place away from all the distractions and get comfortable. Close your eyes and let your thoughts flow freely. This can be quite difficult when you start this exercise, but practice. Practice and stick with it until you learn how to quiet your mind from outside distractions. You will feel refreshed afterwards. You may find this very relaxing.

It is a known fact that thoughts which are often repeated form patterns in the mind that automatically reproduce themselves. Form in your mind a mental picture of yourself succeeding living a prosperous life. Never permit it to fade. Disregard all thoughts of doubt and failure and hold onto your mental image of success. **The mind always tries to complete what it pictures**. So always picture a prosperous life no matter how difficult your current circumstances may be. Whenever a negative thought about your ability to create a prosperous life comes to mind, deliberately voice a positive thought to cancel it out. When a negative thought comes to my mind, I have developed the habit of always voicing out loud: "I rebuke that." I am basically telling my mind I do not agree with that thought and I must think of something better.

An individual will always draw to themselves what they focus on. If we are to attract and have what we desire in life, we must first think it forth. We will always manifest what we think. In order to have success, we must first conceive it in our own thought. Never let doubt creep in for even a minute. Always be positive about yourself and your desires. **Keep watch over the inner working of your thoughts and the law of prosperity will do the rest**.

> "Every thought we think is creating our future." Louise L. Hay

You must surround yourself with a positive atmosphere and keep all negative thoughts that suggest discord, disaster, and failure out of your mind. Hold only to those thoughts, words and pictures which build up and push you toward your vision. Center your attention on what you want and you will automatically draw it to you. You will only get what you accept in life; and if you are not satisfied with your current result, start thinking about your life the way you want it to be. **When you expect great things in your life, you will receive it**. Expect success, love, joy, prosperity, great relationships, health, and good to come to you. By the law of concentration, whatever you dwell upon grows and increases in your life, so think about what you want and keep your mind off what you do not want. Think about what you desire in life.

> "Finally, brethren, whatsoever things are true, whatsoever things are honest, whatsoever things are just, whatsoever things are pure, whatsoever things are lovely, whatsoever things are of good report; if there be any virtue, and if there be any praise, think on these things." Philippians 4:8

Expect lavish abundance in your life every day and you will soon change the character of your entire mind. Every time we focus our thoughts on something, we are producing and creating something; so why not create wealth? Wealth is the result of deliberate thoughts and actions. There is no hit or miss with prosperous living. **To become the master of your destiny, you must learn to control the nature of your dominant, habitual thoughts**.

Key points:

- Be the gardener of your mind; watch what is poured into your mind.

- What you desire is already available to you.

- Be conscious of the abundance within you.

- You are a creator; create what you desire.

- You always get what you focus on.

CHAPTER II
GUARD YOUR MOUTH

CHAPTER II
GUARD YOUR MOUTH

> "Such simple words! But words are mighty things;
> They cast us down, or lift us up to rest;
> They charm and strengthen, till our angel sings
> The last of all the life-songs, and the best."
> **Sarah Doudney**

Words are the most powerful things in the universe. Words are energy and energy is creative. Spoken words program your spirit either for success or defeat, abundance or lack, and hope or despair. You have deep within you the power to fulfill your highest vision of your life. To engage this power you must develop a solid personal relationship with yourself. The ways you think, speak and act contribute to expressing your power or diminishing it.

Have you heard someone continually say they want to be financially free and then in the next sentence confess that they are broke? I once heard someone say, "What you argue for, you keep." You must rise up and have dominion over the lack, poverty and want by speaking words of Truth. **The level of your success begins in your mind and in your mouth**. Many people are unaware that they literally speak things into existence. Their mouth is one of the causes of their circumstances.

Every time you say, "I am broke," "I am stupid" or "I am poor," you are giving power to everything that you are not. Your words are powerful, so speak specific words of wealth for yourself. Speak words of life and not of death. In what direction are your words leading you to? The path of abundance or the path of scarcity?

> "Words and desires go hand in hand... They are moved by the same intention to join together, to communicate, to establish bridges between people, whether they are spoken or written." Laura Esquivel

You need to speak what you desire. You should never underestimate the power of the spoken word. You can actually transform your life by the words that you speak. I remember when I was doing consulting for one of the largest Fortune 500 companies. I had lunch with one of the top executives and asked him, "What does a company look for in a leader when he or she is being considered for one of the top positions in the company?" He said, "We can tell a lot about a person by the words they use." If you listen closely to what someone is truly saying, they will reveal their true character. Those words of wisdom stayed with me. It literally saved me from partnering with some people who lacked integrity in business.

We are the authors of our life and the words we speak form the story everyone sees, reads, and hears. Our thoughts, words, and feelings become flesh and live with us; they become our environment and surround us. In order to create the life you truly desire, you must speak words of faith, power, and victory.

Make it a practice to replace those negative words in your personal vocabulary with positive words. Instead of words of doubt, plant words of hope; instead of words of defeat, plant words of victory; instead of words of fear, plant words of encouragement; instead of words of hate and bitterness, plant and use words of love. If you continue this practice and apply it consistently and persistently every day, you will create a life of true fulfillment. All of the power is in your tongue. So begin speaking the good you desire in your life; learn to speak what your heart desires.

> "Your own words are the bricks and mortar of the dreams you want to realize. Your words are the greatest power you have. The words you choose and their use establish the life you experience." Sonia Choquette

Many people fail at achieving their goals in life because of their words. They put themselves down before they even set out. Sit down with a family member or a friend and have them share with you their dreams, their aspirations, or a goal they always wanted to achieve and ask them why they never took action to accomplish it. They may say something like this: "It's just a dream; I don't think I could really achieve it."

The spoken word has a tremendous impact on both your external and internal reality. **Words are powerful; the words you speak are seeds that produce fruit after their kind**. Whatever you say eventually comes back to you like a boomerang. Just as sure as you plant them, you can be as equally sure a harvest will follow.

Faith vs. Worry According to Hasheem Francis:

You can have what you say when you learn to release faith from the heart in your words. I used to say the word "worry" when I was in college. Every time a professor would make us aware that we were having an exam, my reply was, "I'm not worried about it." But when exam time came around, I found myself worrying.

I did not notice what was causing most of my worries until I got married. My wife Deborah would ask me to do things like pack my clothes the night before a business trip, or get the kids' clothes ready for school, or take the car in for an oil change. I would reply, "I'm not worried about it." Then when the time came, I found myself rushing to pack, or I was not able to find the proper clothes for the kids or the engine light was on in my car. **Because of my words I was being reactive vs. proactive.**

My wife took notice and encouraged me to change what I was saying. She became my accountability partner and when I tell you she held me accountable, there were consequences. As soon as she thought I was going to say the word "worry" she gave me my warning. This is a PG book, so I cannot share my punishment. I will just say I removed that word from my vocabulary immediately. That negative word was keeping me from experiencing peace in my life. I now speak words of faith and victory over my life.

> "Handle them carefully, for words have more power than atom bombs." Pearl Strachan

Every day we must decide to make positive declarations over our lives. Speak words that uplift you, that ignite a fire in you to propel you towards success. You have one life, this is the only chance you have, and there is no retake. God created you to do great things, so declare words of greatness. Your thoughts and words have power to produce the life you give it. **Your words contain energy that brings the fruit of those words back to you**.

Do the words you currently use bring you: abundance or lack, faith or fear, hope or despair?

_____

_____

_____

_____

_____

_____

_____

You were made to achieve the unthinkable; success and wealth desires you more than you know it. The only person who can stop wealth from showing up is you. Your words reveal a great deal about your character. The words you use are the reflection of how you see yourself and life.

Complainers

Do you know someone, a family member, friend or co-worker, who always complains? It does not matter what the subject or the season, all they do is complain. They always find something wrong. It could be a beautiful day and they are complaining about it being too hot. People who complain all of the time are really unhappy people. They are frustrated with the results of their lives and as a consequence, they become critical of everyone and everything around them. They only see life through their foggy, gloomy glasses which obscure their view on situations and people. No one wants to be around a person who has a bad attitude. Life is challenging enough without listening to someone constantly complaining in your ear. Success never comes easy for the complainers and if they do succeed, they will complain about all the hard work it took.

> "If you don't like the way the world is, you change it. You have an obligation to change it, you just do it one step at a time." Marian Wright Edelman

There are two roads—one that leads to prosperity and one that leads to scarcity; they travel in opposite directions. If you desire prosperity, you must with all your heart, mind, and soul refuse to think or speak of any circumstances that lead toward scarcity.

If you study the life of anyone who has achieved success, you will observe that they had control over what went into their mind and the words that came out of their mouth. People who achieve a great deal of success live and honor their words. I remember when I was young and we used to say, "My word is my bond." That meant we stood 100%

behind the words that came out of our mouth. There were no money back guarantees; all you had was your word. **You are a creative, spiritual being: think and speak accordingly. Begin now to speak blessings over everything and everyone who is and comes into your life**. It is just as easy to speak good as it is to condemn and complain.

Your words reveal what is in your heart. When you condemn and complain, you intensify unpleasant conditions in your life. Start speaking words of love, victory, peace, and success in your home, relationships and business. I came to the understanding that before I can expect anyone to say anything positive and encouraging to me, I first must be talking to myself in a positive manner.

The Power of Affirmations

An affirmation is a positive thought spoken aloud and held with the conviction to produce a desired result. As you speak affirmatively, you will develop a new image on the inside and things will begin to change in your favor. Nothing is more powerful and creative than affirmative words. Your words have a positive life force in them when used properly. What we need are affirmations that will empower us, encourage us, and change us for the better, enabling us to go further and reach higher than we ever dreamed possible. Develop the habit of speaking positive, loving, and success-filled messages to yourself.

Exercise: Over the next 21 days, your goal is to develop the habit of speaking positive affirmations to yourself. Each day for the next 21 days, write your positive affirmation and declare it out loud at least three times during the day and night with intense feeling. Continue this until it becomes a part of you; form the habit. The more you hear them, the more you believe they will come to pass. Unless you are fully committed to changing your life, do not start the process. If you do not intend on completing the exercise, do not start. If you do start, go all the way—all out commitment. Make your mind up and do it!

Example: I am a powerful woman. I am Queen. I walk in power.

1. I AM _____
2. I AM _____
3. I AM _____
4. I AM _____
5. I AM _____
6. I AM _____
7. I AM _____
8. I AM _____
9. I AM _____
10. I AM _____
11. I AM _____
12. I AM _____
13. I AM _____
14. I AM _____
15. I AM _____
16. I AM _____
17. I AM _____
18. I AM _____
19. I AM _____
20. I AM _____
21. I AM _____

Commit to it! As you say these faith-filled words, your faith will be strengthened. The more you hear them, the more you will believe that they will surely come to pass. After you have written the affirmation, repeat it over and over with feeling, confidence, belief and enthusiasm so these powerful words can be programmed into your subconscious mind.

These affirmative words will sink from your conscious mind into your subconscious mind and in time, change the way you think. It is your subconscious mind that is the storehouse of your deep-rooted beliefs. To change your circumstances and to attract that which you desire, you must learn to reprogram your subconscious mind. This process will help condition your mind for success. What is important to understand is that your subconscious mind cannot distinguish between fact and fiction. It accepts the images you have constructed while writing and reviewing your affirmations.

If you are willing to invest the time and effort required to develop a new habit of thought, you can become all that you desire. The power of speaking faith into your life delivers your heart's desires to you. It is not enough to think and act on your heart desires; it is important that you declare it aloud. Say it both to yourself and to anyone who will support and encourage you to succeed. You need to keep speaking faith into your life until the results are manifested.

Affirming words of faith into your life truly delivers better results. You may have had setbacks, but it is time for you to start speaking change into your circumstances. As you think and act towards a better prosperous life, add the affirmation aspect to the process. No matter how short or long the journey is, you will surely have what you say.

Whatever the conscious mind believes and accepts, the subconscious mind immediately goes to work to bring into our physical reality. We have to keep talking to ourselves as though we already have what we desire.

Only thoughts with intense feelings bring results. Most people are defeated because they do not commit to personal growth and they believe and confess the wrong things. The defeated speak the words of the enemy, and those words hold them in bondage. Negative statements tend to destroy any good we look to start.

Begin declaring how prosperous and loved you are, and how you are wealthy, healthy, victorious, abundantly supplied, joyful, peaceful, and happy. You deserve better results in your life, so engage in the power of affirming words of faith and you will enjoy a most successful life. Your confessions will change your life. Your words give your life focus and attention.

Key points:

- Your tongue holds the power of life and death.

- You are the author of your life and your words create the story.

- Speak positive declarations daily.

- Speak words of Truth, Faith and Victory.

- You can have what you say.

Life

Life is an opportunity, benefit from it.
Life is a beauty, admire it.
Life is a dream, realize it.
Life is a challenge, meet it.
Life is a duty, complete it
Life is a game, play it.
Life is a promise, fulfill it.
Life is sorrow, overcome it.
Life is a song, sing it.
Life is a struggle, accept it.
Life is a tragedy, confront it.
Life is an adventure, dare it.
Life is luck, make it.
Life is life, fight for it!"

Mother Teresa

CHAPTER III
MY ATTITUDE IS EITHER MY FRIEND OR FOE

CHAPTER III
MY ATTITUDE IS EITHER MY FRIEND OR FOE

> "The greatest discovery of all time is that a person can change their future by merely changing their attitude."
> Oprah Winfrey

Your attitude affects all areas of your life. Our attitude comes from our expectations about life. If we expect things to be wonderful, we will have a positive attitude. If we expect things to turn out for the worst, things have a tendency to turn out that way. Your attitude is the most visible manifestation of you as a person. A positive mental attitude is the driving force that will assist you as you set out to achieve all that you desire in life. It takes discipline to consistently have a positive attitude, especially when you are dealing with difficult people or situations.

You will be challenged, but the challenges come to strengthen your attitude. When you can smile in the face of opposition and keep a positive attitude no matter what the circumstances are around you, then you have fully developed an attitude that will propel you toward success. I know you may be thinking to yourself, "Yeah, right. Do you smile every time you are faced with a difficult situation?" And my answer is, "Not all the time; it is a work in progress. I am human just like you." There are times when I do not feel like being positive; I call those days: "Oh, woe is me days." But I learned and it took time and discipline to not allow myself to get stuck with a negative attitude.

I also have an accountability partner who holds me responsible when I am in that negative state. My accountability partner is quick to call me on it. I may not want to hear what she has to say, but I know she has my best interest at heart.

The most successful people view their attitude as a valuable asset that deserves protection and attention. Most often, people with a negative attitude do not get far in life. Their attitude about life holds them back and they become what you would call "a light dimmer." As soon as they walk in the room the lights dim; they drain all the positive energy in the room with their attitude. Successful people stay clear of people with a negative attitude. Have you ever spent time with someone who constantly complains about everything and as soon as you leave them you find yourself complaining. When we share time with others, our attitude often sets the tone for how we treat one another.

There is nothing in life as dangerous as a negative attitude. No one who was negative about themselves and their opportunities in life has ever achieved lasting success. You must learn to cast negative destructive thinking aside and focus on the positive. One of the steps to developing a positive attitude is to become aware of your current attitude. In order to succeed in building a life filled with prosperity, you need to approach life with a positive or affirmative attitude.

A positive mental attitude is an absolute must to achieve success. The quality of your life will depend mostly on your attitude. An optimistic attitude attracts optimistic people. A negative, constantly complaining attitude attracts negative, constantly complaining people. Until you change your thought pattern, it will continue to form your attitude which will be the prevailing way you choose to see the world throughout your life, causing you to strictly limit your life's vision and impose tight boundaries around your beliefs.

Your life is affected by your habit of thinking and attitude of mind. Your attitude is a composite of your thoughts, feelings and actions. The only way you can improve the results you are getting in life is to take full responsibility for your attitude, only then will you be able to improve your results. All of your actions are unconsciously influenced by your thoughts, thus helping to bring into manifestation or attracting to you an environment that corresponds to your thoughts. This is why the quality of your thinking is so instrumental in forming your world view and it explains why the most successful people guard their thoughts, and take the time to think about what they are thinking about.

Your attitude reflects your thoughts. Your attitude is either your friend or foe. Attitude is the criterion for success. Developing a positive or negative attitude is a choice. No one can give you a great attitude, it is something you must develop for yourself. It would be great to borrow a positive attitude on those difficult days. You will always see your attitude reflected back to you in the faces and the behaviors of the people around you. If you have a positive, optimistic attitude, people will respond to you almost immediately, even before you open your mouth, in a positive and cheerful way.

Make Your Life A Masterpiece

If you desire to make your life a masterpiece, then you need to have the right attitude about different areas of life. Your real change in life comes from within. It is your own attitude that demands your focus. The key to prosperity is to change your thoughts and attitudes about yourself and your success. It takes time to design the life you desire. Most people want a quick fix and when something they desire does not come immediately, they quit. Successful women never quit. When they suffer a setback, they just pick themselves up and keep going.

Attitude and Goal Setting

Women who excel in life are those who produce results, not excuses. Anybody can come up with excuses and explanations for why she hasn't made it. You will see your desires come to pass if you believe and refuse to give up. Remember to not let the delays in achieving your goals affect your attitude. A delay is not a denial. **How would you feel if you told everyone that you were going to be financially free in one year and you did not achieve that goal? Would you feel like a failure or would you continue to go after your goal?**

Fear of failure keeps many from taking necessary risks, but the willingness to take risks and step out on faith is a measure of your prosperity consciousness. **One way to overcome fear is to ask yourself, "What is the worst thing that could happen if I failed at something I really wanted?"** If you can live with the worst possible results, then get out there and go for it. Our highs in life come not from having or surmounting any single challenge but from the strength we experience when we find the means within us to face a challenge and overcome the barriers to resolution. We get energy when we take risks and act in spite of our fears.

> "I discovered I always have choices and sometimes it's only a choice of attitude." Judith M. Knowlton

Since your thoughts influence your attitude, it is essential to continually work to improve your quality of thinking. To develop a positive attitude towards wealth, family, health and prosperity, we need to take an assessment of your current attitude.

Describe the attitude you have about yourself? What do you see when you look in the mirror? Do you love yourself?

What type of person would your family and friends describe you as?

What is your attitude toward prosperity and those who are prosperous?

Do you believe a woman of great wealth achieved her success through honesty, integrity, and commitment, or through greed and by taking advantage of others? Why?

When I began to develop a prosperity consciousness, my attitude was that I was going to be kind, loving, generous, happy and wealthy. I did not want to be like the wealthy people displayed on television. When I was growing up, the pictures I recalled of the wealthy was through various television programs we watched in our home on a regular basis such as *Duck Tales* with Scrooge McDuck, who was a miserable individual; Mr. Howell from *Gilligan's Island*, who was snobby; and Mr. George Jefferson from *The Jefferson's*, who was rude.

Once I got to really know wealthy people, I realized they were nothing like what I had seen or heard. They were some of the most kind-hearted people who were doing a great deal of philanthropic work around the country. It is truly amazing how we allow others who do not have full knowledge or wealth to dictate our attitude toward wealth.

Your attitude governs the way you act, the way the action will unfold, and the reward or consequences of your action. You must continuously examine your personal attitude toward wealth because it has a huge impact on your life. **Your attitude is what separates you from the crowd**. It is easy to live and be a part of the crowd; just watch what they watch, talk how they talk, read what they read, do what they do and you will get what they got. To get the results you desire and live abundantly, you must do everything you can to separate yourself from those who will pull you down while you develop your dream.

> "We are all here for some special reason. Stop being a prisoner of your past. Become the architect of your future." Robin Sharma

Your attitude is shaped by many factors: personality, environment, self-image, the positive or negative expressions of others and your thoughts. No matter what you seek to achieve, your attitude is a vital part of that success. Your attitude about yourself, your potential, your ability, and your unique capacity to achieve will, in a large part, set the limits on what you do achieve.

Attitude of Gratitude:

The best attitude you can possibly desire to express is one of gratitude and appreciation for the things you value most in life. By being grateful for what you currently already have in your life attracts more good to you. When you are grateful, you open the door for abundance to flow. By focusing your thoughts and attention on the abundance that is already present in your life, you can create a positive attitude that will attract more to be grateful for. Keep in mind that feeling prosperous is enjoying fully what you already have. Right now, all of us have resources we are not using—resources that can be appreciated. **A thankful heart is one that has taken the time to count the blessings**. Take a moment and really feel the emotion of gratitude.

> "Keep a grateful journal. Every night, list five things that you are grateful for. What it will begin to do is change your perspective of your day and your life." Oprah Winfrey

What 5 Things Are You Grateful For?

_____
_____
_____
_____
_____

Part of your success depends upon your gratitude and recognition that God is your source. God is the one who supplies everything you need. Anything good in your life is a blessing from God. Living with an attitude of gratitude is without a doubt the best way to live life. **I am grateful you have committed to being all that God created you to be!**

Attitude of Giving

What is your attitude about giving? Are you a cheerful giver?

_____
_____
_____
_____
_____
_____
_____
_____

As you give, so shall you receive. If you do not sow, you cannot reap. In all of life, receiving depends upon giving. Some women feel they have nothing to give.

Most people think giving is only about money, but there is love, joy, laughter, and encouragement you also can give.

The only way to experience a harvest is to be a sower. If you sow love you will reap love, sow finances and you will reap finances. If you desire more money to meet your needs, be a generous money-sower and in due season, you will reap a harvest. When you become a giver, you automatically move yourself into the realm of a receiver. There are no exceptions to this rule. This is the law of sowing and reaping. You will receive everything that you give. **"Give, and it shall be given unto you…" (Luke 6:38).**

Begin to understand your God-given right of giving. If you will do so, there will come a day when the prosperity of God will literally overtake you. You will have more than enough to share with others with plenty left over to meet you and your family's every need. When you are a cheerful giver, God will bless you and give you back many blessings out of His abundance!

Key points:

- Your attitude will determine your level of success.

- A positive or a negative attitude is a choice.

- Read positive books; there are plenty at the library and it is a free membership.

- Make a habit of sharing and giving to others.

- Hold loving thoughts toward yourself and others.

- Limit your time talking to, watching, or listening to negative information (i.e. doom and gloom friends, the news, or moody music).

CHAPTER IV
WHOSE REPORT DO YOU BELIEVE?

CHAPTER IV
WHOSE REPORT DO YOU BELIEVE?

> "It is this belief in a power larger than myself and other than myself, which allows me to venture into the unknown and even the unknowable." Maya Angelou

The impossible begins to happen when a positive attitude evolves into belief. The beliefs we have about ourselves and life are responsible for who we ultimately become and what we eventually achieve in life. What you believe to be true is true and nothing else. Belief is the power behind our creative thoughts. Thought alone is not enough to manifest an idea into physical reality, it must be combined with belief. Every aspect of your life, from the state of your health to the state of your relationships and your finances, is accurately revealing your thoughts and your beliefs.

Before we can begin to create a vision for what it is we want to do in life, we first must have the belief that we have the capability to achieve whatever it is we desire. Without this belief, we would never even attempt to do anything about our dreams. Not manifesting our dreams is like the song from Otis Redding, "We'll be sitting on the dock of the bay, watching the tides roll away, wasting time." Success begins with a state of mind. You must believe you'll be successful in order to become a success.

Are you an optimist or pessimist?

The difference between an optimist and a pessimist is that the optimist mindset is, "I will see it when I believe it." The pessimist says, "I will believe it when I see it" Optimists seem to have different ways of dealing with the world that set them apart from the average. They keep their mind on what they want and keep looking for ways to get it.

> **"No pessimist ever discovered the secret of the stars, or sailed to an uncharted land, or opened a new doorway for the human spirit." Helen Keller**

The reason why some women may not believe in themselves is that they may be holding on to past mistakes. Realize that if you do not let go of past failures, frustrations or rejection, then you simply are not available to create your future with more productive levels of thinking that lead to more effective action and results. **We cannot go and relive the past; the focus must be on today and today only**.

If you study the life of women who have achieved success or have had a huge impact on the life of others, you will see that many have made mistakes and had setbacks but continued to pursue their goals. When they experienced setbacks, their mind held the belief of their end result, accomplishing what they set out to do. Today is your day to create your success. Your today and your future begin right now. Your past does not determine your future; you have the power to change your life into what you desire it to be.

You have no reason to doubt your worth or potential as a woman. God does not doubt you, so your confidence should be paramount. You have only to accept the reality of your real self. In every arena of life, there are women who are successful and women who are unsuccessful. What makes the difference can be summarized in one word: belief. Belief is one of the most important elements in achieving your life's desires. Your beliefs are powerful. They make up the woman you will become and influence what you will achieve in life. In order to succeed in life you must absolutely believe beyond a shadow of a doubt that you have the ability to achieve whatever you have set out to do.

What is it that rich, successful, and prosperous women possess that others may not? They believe in themselves and their God-given abilities. They respect themselves and earn the respect of others. Respecting yourself begins with the knowledge of who you are and what is important to you as a woman.

Take for instance Martha Stewart; she firmly believes in the Martha Stewart brand and the quality of her products so much that other companies pay her millions of dollars just to put the name "Martha Stewart" on their products. It all began with her belief in herself, the Martha Stewart brand, and her mission to provide some of the most elegant home products across the country.

What is the difference between you and Martha Stewart? You may be thinking a couple million dollars. She was not born a millionaire; she went out and created a brand that earned her millions of dollars. Confidence comes when you pursue your dreams and passions. Studies show that women who enjoy their life usually feel good about who they are.

> "It's totally out of desire and totally out of belief that - not that I am essential, but that I am still a vibrant, wise human being with great dreams for the future, great hopes for the future, a great team to work with and a really great company to be involved with... I mean, this is my life." Martha Stewart

In life, people are going to tell you that you cannot achieve the dreams you have set out to accomplish. They will tell you that you do not have the ability, potential, skill, or drive. This is the "crabs in the barrel mentality." Those people who say you cannot achieve your dreams have to keep you down because your success will eliminate their excuses for not being successful. If you listen to them, you will not succeed, you will fail. Do not listen to cynics and dream-killers. Do not listen to those who do not believe in you. Listen to what God says about you and tell yourself that you will succeed and you will achieve what you set out to do. It takes preparation, knowledge, persistence and work, but you can do anything you set out to do if you believe in yourself. **Be your own #1 fan!**

To develop belief in yourself and your greatest potential of living a prosperous life, you will have to overcome difficulties and doubt, and push yourself beyond any level you may have achieved in the past. You Can Do It! All the tools you need are available to you.

History is often written by people who believe in a dream so intensely that they are willing to commit themselves totally to the realization of that dream. You have probably heard it said before, "It is impossible to succeed without believing." In other words, if you want to succeed in life, then you must believe in what you are doing. It is called Faith and with it, your possibilities in life are limitless. Without faith, well, the complete opposite is true and it leads you down a pathway of failure every time. Once you come to the complete understanding of the level of abundance God has planned for you, you can rise out of your current situation and reach a far more prosperous level. No matter where you are now, it is time for you to move to a new dimension of living. God has a divine plan for your life. Begin now to elevate your thoughts to a new level, seeking Godly wisdom to guide you into a new level of plenty.

> "You must know that you are worth much to yourself whether you accomplish anything or not. Even if you are rejected in the world's eyes, you are valuable to yourself."
> Deborah Francis

When you succeed in convincing your subconscious mind that you are wealthy, you believe you deserve to be wealthy and it feels good to be wealthy, your subconscious mind will automatically seek ways of making your feelings of wealth manifest in material form. **The world as you see it is only a reflection of who you are.**

Be willing to let go of the mental belief patterns and behaviors that have resulted in your living a life that is less than what you have always dreamed. You must look in the mirror when you ask who is responsible for your triumph or let down. As long as you are persistent in your pursuit of your vision, you will continue to grow. **You cannot choose the day or time when the vision will come to pass; have faith and believe it will happen on its own time**.

Believe with all of your heart that you will do what you were made to do. Once your mind has formed the habit of holding joyous, happy, prosperous pictures, it will not be easy to form the opposite habit. Believe that you are governed by God, and that you are directed by Divine guidance. Know that everything you think, say or do that is constructive is done through Divine authority. Have faith in your God-given power to be prosperous in life. Focus your efforts on achieving your desires and nothing on earth will keep you from it.

Believe in Yourself!

When you believe that you will prosper, you will. If you believe that you will win, you will! If you believe you will be wealthy, you will be wealthy. It is evident that you will become like the person you think and believe you are and achieve only what you think and believe you are capable of. The person who has acquired the power of keeping their mind filled with the thoughts of gratitude, abundance, power, confidence, and wealth, which uplift and encourage, has solved one of the great mysteries of life. **When you develop yourself to the point where your belief in yourself is so strong that you know you can accomplish anything you put your mind to, you open the door to unlimited possibilities**. You are capable of functioning in a power and might to where nothing can stop you. Even when the going gets rough, you must have belief that your vision will come to pass. You have to continue to use your faith.

Whenever you think of yourself, always hold the image of yourself as you would intend it to be. Do not dwell upon your imperfections or weaknesses, because that will distort your image. Hold tenaciously to the idea of yourself in your perfection as the personality God intended you to be. It takes faith and patience to bring these God-given principles to their fullest potential. You must regularly plant your seeds. At first, your sowing may look futile. However, there will come a day when the harvest will begin to come in such abundance that you will have more than enough.

You have a purpose in this life; God created you to be the best you. Have the courage to change on the inside and know you will be the great person God called you to be. Some of the world's most successful individuals throughout time have accomplished what they set out to do; they believed in themselves even when others did not. Wealthy and successful people understand that there are no shortcuts in life.

Focus more on your desires than on your doubts and the dream will take care of itself. Your doubts are not as powerful as your desires unless you make them so. Believe in yourself. This is an important step because without the belief in yourself, you will not have the courage to pursue your goals.

Key points

- Your belief is your power.

- Be Your Own #1 Fan.

- Do not listen to the cynics and dream-killers.

- You will become what you believe you will be.

Key point to practice:

- Visualize and carry yourself with a self-confident air and you will not only inspire others with a belief in your ability to become prosperous, but you will also come to believe yourself.

CHAPTER V
CREATING AN INSPIRED VISION

CHAPTER V
CREATING AN INSPIRED VISION

> "Protect your vision at all cost. Commitment is the willingness to do whatever it takes to bring your vision to reality. Never be ashamed of what God has accomplished through YOU!"
> **Deborah Francis**

A successful woman is able to visualize her dream and then make it a reality. Do you have a dream that you can visualize? Do you have a vision for your life or are you functioning on auto pilot aimlessly? **A vision is not seen as a dream but a reality that has not come into existence**. Your vision should include who you want to be, what you want to do and what you want to have. It is important to know clearly who you are right now and to know who you want to become. This includes your habits, attitudes, and points of view. If you are unclear about yourself, you will be unclear about your future.

When creating a vision, you should know where you are starting and your desired end result. Everything done by human beings first comes into existence by a vision. Only afterward is it translated into the external world. Nothing can be created or accomplished without an idea, a picture, an image, or a sense of the thing first occurring in the mind. Imagine getting in your car with your family and saying you are going on a family trip but you have no idea where you are going; you just know you are going somewhere. A trip like this would cost you time and money. It is unlikely that you would find a destination you like if you do not know where you are going.

Your family may have some concerns about you due to the lack of navigation and vision. If you do not have a clear picture of your destination and a precise, detailed map to get there, you will never arrive no matter how hard you try.

I have heard some women complain about being too busy with their daily routine to plan for a better life, much less look ahead, even though they wish their circumstances were better; and we all know wishing gets you nowhere. I think the truth is not that these women are so busy that they cannot plan for a better life but that they are working so hard so they do not have to look at their life and make necessary changes.

Fear of failure, peer pressure and discomfort at the thought of leaving their routine lulled them to settle instead of going for what they truly desire. They would rather spend 8 to 10 hours on a job they do not like and then come home and spend 4 hours in front of the idiot box to escape their mental prison.

In their waning years, they will be racked with the pain of regret and haunted by the words: "could have, should have, if only I would have." You are not going to go down that path; you have come too far to turn back now. Even if you do not achieve all your desires, it is what happens to you as a person in the process of going after your dream that is truly valuable.

> "Set your sights high, the higher the better. Expect the most wonderful things to happen, not in the future but right now. Realize that nothing is too good. Allow absolutely nothing to hamper you or hold you up in any way." Eileen Caddy

It is about the journey. It is what you become that fulfills you, not what you get. There are two ways you can fail at living your most fulfilling life: not truly believing in your vision and limiting yourself in what you think you can achieve—basically selling yourself short.

You are Built To Prosper, so there is no time for small thinking. You will never know how far you can go in life until you get up and set sail toward your vision. I urge you to pick the first route to 'failure' because it is only in going farther than you think which shows you how far you can go. **Think Big. Aim High. Go Strong.**

Are you ready to achieve the unthinkable? Well, begin now to visualize the life you want to live. You will get whatever you visualize and work for. If you keep up this practice and apply it each day of your life, you will find that it will produce the greatness of success and wealth you desire. It is a matter of concentration, preparation, and focusing all your power in order to attract your dreams into reality. Visualizing is also the natural process by which the mind communicates deeply buried feelings and beliefs.

The importance of making this process conscious is that without awareness, we usually choose to act according to the way we envision reality around us, not necessarily the way it actually is. Visualize the able, earnest, useful, fruitful and prospering person you want to be. It all begins in your mind. **Renew your mind daily**. As you plan to prosper, give yourself the gift of self-discipline. It is a willingness to listen to your inner voice that demands excellence instead of being average. Begin by creating your ideal life.

Having a vision might be the most powerful way to keep you focused on what you want in life while keeping you motivated in achieving it. Vision will open up your mind to many possibilities of a greater and brighter future. When you can envision a future that is better, happier, and more productive, you are more likely to make the changes that are necessary for you to reach that experience in life. Before you can become the woman you desire or before you can have what you want, you must first see yourself achieving it.

> "Don't live down to expectations. Go out there and do something remarkable." Wendy Wasserstein

You must see yourself as prosperous. You must have a vivid picture in your mind as to what living prosperous means. The mind thinks in pictures.

Whatever your intentions are for living a prosperous life, it is time to get it out in the open in as much detail as possible. The time is now to create your vision. Find yourself somewhere quiet where you can formulate your thoughts. We are going to design the life you desire. Knowing what you want in life is a reward in itself. When you truly know what you want in life, it puts you in a different league. It is not always easy to sit down and design your life; we were never taught how to do that in school. Believe me, if you take the time to visualize what you want and be as specific as possible, those things you desire will draw closer to you.

Putting your desires in writing is an important step toward bringing your vision and thoughts into manifestation. Did you know that writing is one of the keys to manifestation?

What Is Your Vision For Your Life?

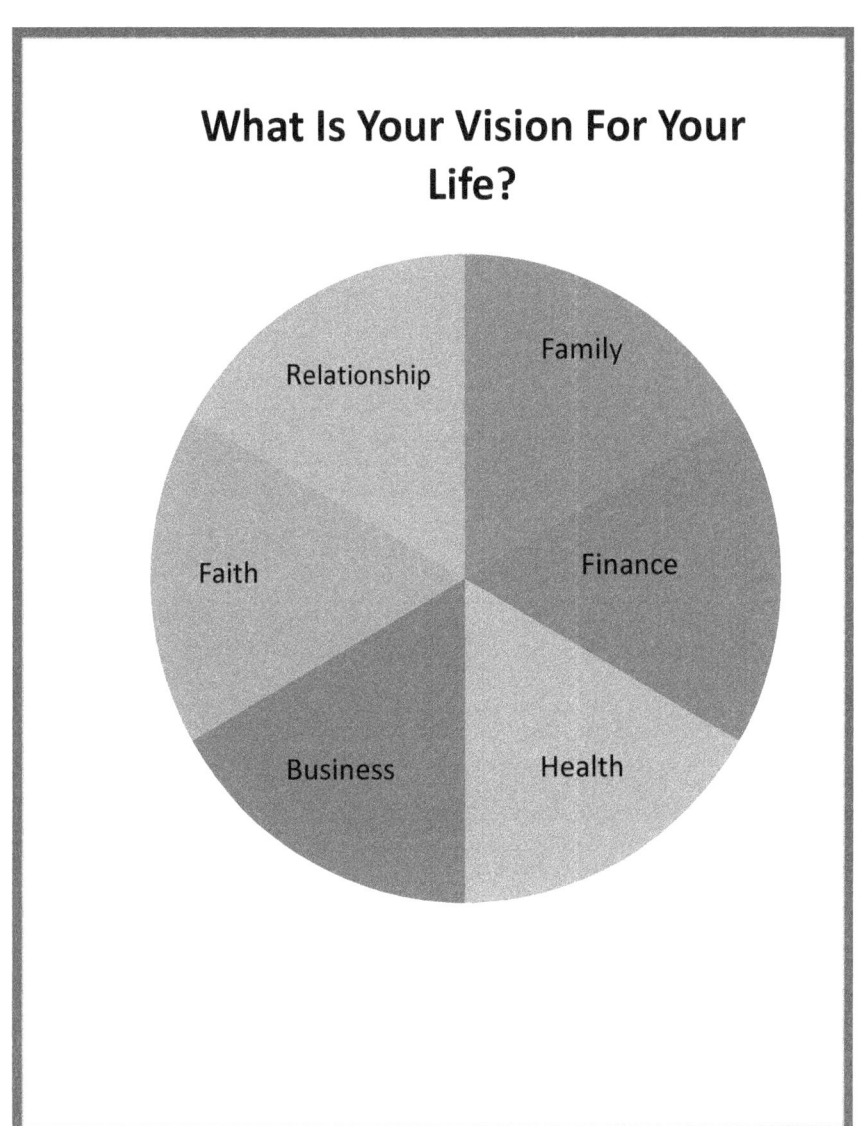

Describe in great detail your vision for each area of your life. Write it in the present tense as if you have it right now. Write it down in full detail and in living color.

Faith: _____

_____
_____
_____
_____
_____
_____
_____
_____
_____
_____
_____
_____
_____
_____
_____
_____
_____
_____
_____
_____
_____
_____
_____
_____

Family:

Health:

Career/ Business: _____

Finance:

Love/Purpose: _____

Relationships: _____

How will you feel when you are succeeding in life and all your financial needs are taken care of?

Describe what a perfect day would be like for you:

Once you have completed your "vision creation" assignment, it is time to feel a sense of accomplishment. Now you know what you desire in life and it is written down. You have just designed your life. **Hold this mental vision of a prosperous life you created firmly in your mind, and it will actually happen if you continually affirm it in your thoughts and you work diligently to make it happen**. Always visualize the outcome of the goals as you wish to experience them. The more you can see yourself achieving the goals, the quicker they will become a reality. If you learn to mix emotion along with the visualization, this will speed up the process as well. Your main purpose is to be absolutely clear about what it is you want, make a plan to achieve that goal, and then think about it and work on it every single day. Do not settle for anything less.

Create a Dream Board

> "Every great dream begins with a dreamer. Always remember, you have within you the strength, the patience, and the passion to reach for the stars to change the world." Harriet Tubman

You have invested the time in writing out your desires, but the mind thinks in pictures so it needs visuals. Dream-building involves creating a physical representation of what you want to achieve. Your dream board will represent how you visualize the achievement of your goals and your journey toward that achievement. Look through magazines and find pictures that represent your vision. Get pictures of the beautiful home you plan on living in, get pictures of your family, find pictures that represent success and cut them out and place them on a board. This will be your own personal dream board. If you are married, make this a family activity. Have some fun with this! We currently have five dream boards in our home. (We dream big in our house.) Once you complete your dream boards place them where you will see them regularly. It will help motivate and inspire you toward achieving your goals.

Back in Chapter II, you created 21 positive affirmations. Add these affirmations to your dream board. In time, you will become a more definite, positive, focused, optimistic, creative, and determined person. The more you become, the more you will begin to activate all of your mind's power and organize all the mental laws to work on your behalf. You will be achieving at a higher level than you ever have before.

Key points:

- Think big; there is no room for small thinking.
- Enjoy the process in developing your vision.
- Practice visualizing your goals daily.
- Your mind thinks in pictures. Dream big.

Key points to practice:

- Focus on your vision daily.
- Review your written vision once a day.

CHAPTER VI
DECIDE OR BE CONFORMED

CHAPTER VI
DECIDE OR BE CONFORMED

> "As you become more clear about who you really are, you will be better able to decide what is best for you - the first time around." Oprah Winfrey

You do not have a problem to solve, you simply have a decision to make. Our decisions set the course of our life. If you had a choice to continue down your current path and live the exact life you are living right now or to make a decision that would change everything, which would you choose? **Until a decision is made and acted upon, nothing happens.** No one can decide for you. If you want to control the direction of your life, you must develop the habit of making good decisions. Making wise decisions is one of life's greatest challenges. **It is not what you do once in a while that has an impact on the direction of your life, it is what you do consistently. Decide today that you are not going to live in mediocrity.**

For you to get the results you desire in life, it is imperative to decide what results you are committed to and know specifically how these results will change your life. It is critical to decide what kind of woman you are committed to becoming. Get clear about what you want to be, do, and have and what your life will be like after you accomplish this. With clarity, you will find it becomes easier to make the kind of decisions that will move you in the direction you desire. The circumstances we face in life are due to our past decisions.

The future events we may experience depend upon the kind of decisions we make today.

Life is made up of little and big decisions and how a woman decides determine the course of her life. Women who are successful in life know how to make decisions. If you do not learn how to make good decisions, you will continue to have the kind of results you had up until now. Deciding creates the purpose; it gives you a goal—a reason to do what you do. Once a decision is made, carrying it out becomes a matter of will and courage and dedication.

> "You may be disappointed if you fail, but you are doomed if you don't try." Beverly Sills

Make a decision today to develop yourself to the point where you can achieve your personal goals and become everything you are capable of becoming. Be diligent in your decisions, write your goals down, make sure you look at them every day, then ponder ways you can possibly achieve these goals. Determine exactly what you want to be able to do. Decide who you want to become. Describe exactly what you will look like when you become successful in your personal life and business. **Your decision to live a prosperous life is not an overnight success; there is some work that is required**.

No matter what difficulties may arise, no matter how much harder your work may be more than you anticipated, do not waiver or turn back. Those who whine and complain about how life is so unfair are simply increasing their own trouble. Until that woman realizes that the cause of all of her troubles are due to the decisions she made in life, she cannot make the necessary changes that will lead her toward a life of success. Her thoughts, ideals, and attitude about life must all become transformed.

The Apostle Paul stated in Romans 12:2, **"Be ye transformed by the renewing of your mind."**

Set your face toward your goals; never permit anyone or anything to undermine your destiny. Saturate your mind with thoughts of success, wealth, health, and prosperity. You can become who you want and have what you desire if you make the decision to think on it. It may take some time before your desires physically manifest in your life; be patient, you will not be denied. Most women have already decided to follow the masses. These women are being conformed. It is easy to do what everyone else is doing. It is easy to sit in front of a television (Tell You Their Vision) for three hours and not work on building a relationship with your spouse or children. It is easy to not go to the gym and workout. It is very easy for a college student to put off doing an important research paper and go party with their friends. I know this because I have done it myself. My favorite line was if everyone else is "not" doing it, why should I?

In order to gain control over your life, you must take your power back and learn how to allow yourself to be what you have envisioned. You are responsible for ruling your own actions and decisions. To make consistently good decisions, take the right action when needed; refraining from the wrong action requires character and self-discipline. Society has been programmed to be dependent, not independent. Many believe and have decided that they will gain wealth through dependency instead of independence. They are seeking handouts not hand-ups.

> "There's always something to suggest that you'll never be who you wanted to be. Your choice is to take it or keep on moving." **Phylicia Rashad**

We are taught to depend on the government to take care of us when we get old through a social security check. The masses are taught to keep working a job they hate just for a steady paycheck. Then you have those who are hoping someday to win the lotto. This is not independent thinking because the power belongs to that which you depend on. Who sold us on that plan?

If you read this far, I know you will make the wise decision and not be conformed. It is your life to live and make count. Wealth and great prosperity await you. **Decide today that you will be all that God created you to be**. Venture out. Refuse to stay in the valley of mediocrity.

Key points:

- Make the decision to be prosperous and act on it.
- Do not be conformed by the negative opinions of other people.
- It is your life to live; make it count.

CHAPTER VII
ARE YOU COMMITTED TO THE CAUSE?

CHAPTER VII
ARE YOU COMMITTED TO THE CAUSE?

> "Don't urge me to leave you or to turn back from you. Where you go I will go, and where you stay I will stay. Your people will be my people and your God my God. Where you die I will die, and there I will be buried. May the LORD deal with me, be it ever so severely, if anything but death separates you and me."
> **The Book of Ruth**

I have personally created a prosperous life and have observed many women who have reached this level and beyond. My observation is that there is nothing magical about it; it is a choice of all out commitment. **Prosperity, success or riches do not necessarily go to the most talented or gifted but to those who are the most committed.**

The difference between average living and prosperous living is a matter of commitment. Are you committed to creating a life filled with prosperity? Those who have a high prosperity consciousness simply make commitments to achieve greater goals. Fear of the unknown is one of the greatest obstacles that you will face when you are traveling on the journey toward a prosperous life.

A worthwhile goal can never be achieved without encountering failure, criticism, obstacles and roadblocks.

Your greatness will be molded and measured by the mountains you choose to conquer. And there will be some mountains you will definitely need to overcome, such as fear of failure and any limiting beliefs that may be holding you back from achieving the life you desire.

Worthwhile goals are always found on the top of rugged mountains, never on valley floors. **You must overcome your fear of failure in order to achieve your dreams. Fear of failure is the enemy of your success.** Failure is not a disaster; it is an event in which you did not achieve your desired outcome.

You can learn more from your failure than you can from your success; it can make you wiser. If you read the autobiography of anyone who has achieved great success, you will see that they had to overcome some great failures to achieve their dreams. Many successful women had to overcome bankruptcy, failed marriages, and negative addictive habits.

Failure became their greatest teacher and mentor. Every woman has within them the ability to accomplish great things because of their determination to learn, improve, emulate and change. Change demands self-discipline, so you must command yourself and make yourself do what needs to be done. If you desire a better life than what you have now, you must learn to overcome all fears and obstacles that stand in your way.

Fear can be a tyrannical dictator that drastically limits or even destroys your hopes and dreams. Many people may experience fear when they are moving outside of their comfort zone. **Remember: There is no wealth inside the comfort zone.** Step outside of what has become comfortable and familiar. You must risk losing control in order to push yourself into the outer limits of your abilities. It is the way to a prosperous life.

Women who see themselves as failures or have a low self-esteem will eventually fail regardless of their best effort to succeed. While women who see themselves as prosperous, successful and confident will eventually create the life they desire regardless of how many mountains they may have to climb or run through. They succeed because they are committed to the process.

Those who succeed in their undertakings are those who set their faces toward their goal and with unwavering conviction, affirm and reaffirm their confidence in their ability to reach it.

God did not make us to be a failure. He made us to be and to live prosperously. Expect the best; you must put your whole heart into what you want to accomplish. People are defeated in life not because they lack ability, but because they lack faith in their abilities. They do not wholeheartedly expect to prosper.

If you are a woman who wants to win in every aspect of your life, being committed to the process must be ingrained in your subconscious mind. A major key to success in life, to getting whatever you really desire, is to have the mindset of "I will, until…" Whatever you are going to do, give it your all. Hold nothing back. I have created the mindset that **"I will consistently persist until I achieve my desired outcome."** What is your mindset about keeping commitments and being persistent in achieving your goals? We all have the same 24 hours in a day.

Once you make the commitment to make the necessary changes in life, distractions will come and they will come by the truck load. The difference between the women who achieve success and those who do not is that those who are successful know how to make the most of their 24 hours. No one has complete control over their daily life; someone or something always seems to be pulling us in many directions. But you must develop the habit of saying "no" to things that waste time and are not priorities.

One way to use your time wisely is to cut down on activities that do not move you forward toward your goal. **To effectively manage yourself within time, you need to set goals. When you know where you are going, you can then figure out what exactly needs to be done and in what order.** Without proper goal-setting, you will waste your time on confusing and conflicting priorities. People tend to neglect goal-setting because it requires time and effort. What they fail to consider is that a little time and effort put in now saves an enormous amount of time, effort and frustration in the future.

Learn to say "No" to tasks and people that are a distraction. This is not being selfish, this is called being focused and committed. Planning helps you increase your useful time. When you have a plan and it is written on paper, it will more than likely keep you committed, and it will be your blueprint on how to get from where you are to where you desire to be. Prioritizing what needs to be done is especially important.

Without it, you may work hard but you will not achieve the results you desire because what you are working on is not of strategic importance. Most people have a "to-do" list of some sort. The problem with many of these lists is they are just a list of activities that need to get done. There is no rhyme or reason to the list and because of this, the work they do is just as unstructured. To work efficiently, you need to work on the most important, highest-value tasks.

My business partners and I meet once a month to discuss the company's monthly goals and review our annual goals. One person is assigned to keep record of our discussions. We address any new product ideas or services we intend to bring to the market and we also discuss each team member's monthly goals. At the end of the meeting, we all receive an email with everything we discussed. Now it is each team member's responsibility to include their goals in their daily or monthly planner. So when the team meets at the beginning of the following month, we can go over our goals; and if someone has not achieved a goal, we can always go back to the team member's daily activity to see if that person was utilizing his or her time effectively.

Take Responsibility

As you go on this journey, you must take responsibility for your life. By taking responsibility for your life, you have control. You no longer live a life of blame. Those who live a life of blame live in a mental prison; they give all their power to outside circumstances. Those circumstances hold the key to their freedom.

If you learn to fully accept the responsibility for where you are right now despite your past mistakes, you will be empowered by one of the foundational principles of success. The prosperous spirit within you cannot be honed or harnessed if you cannot accept and take total responsibility for your life. You see, if you are stuck in the blame mode, you cannot get to where you desire to go.

Those who take responsibility for the results in their life stick with their vision; and if the actions they are implementing are not getting them the results they desire, they become flexible. They are not afraid of change. They give it their all. On your journey, you will face unexpected situations but you must stay the course. I never met or read about anyone who achieved great success and did not come up against some sort of opposition. It is part of the development process. Great success does not come easy. **It takes commitment and sacrifice and the more ambitious the goal, the greater the sacrifice**.

Do you know what you want to do? What career path do you want to take? What brings you joy? You need to know what you want to do, why you want to do it and a have a plan of action on how to go about achieving your goals. You need to know the benefits of taking action and the negative consequences for not taking action. Acquiring clarity and increasing effectiveness will accelerate your success.

Most people get excited about their dreams and goals in the infant stages of planning but once any setbacks come, they quit. This is the main reason why most successful people say it is lonely at the top and crowded at the bottom. Some women are not committed; they will not participate in their own rescue. It simply takes too much commitment and sacrifice to achieve a great level of success.

I know I will probably lose a couple of readers with that last statement. Some women are afraid of these two words: commitment and sacrifice. The lack of understanding of these two words has been the cause of many failed marriages and business opportunities. **In order to achieve your goals in life, it will take commitment, sacrifice, perseverance and discipline**. Perseverance is the ability to keep going despite the circumstances.

People who live a life of blame give up easily, but those who take responsibility stay the course. They focus on the things that are important. If they are not sure, they seek the counsel of those who have achieved success in their area of need. When seeking counsel, you must put your pride aside and not be afraid to ask for guidance.

When you take responsibility for the results you get in life, you will no longer settle for mediocrity. Your standards will change and you will begin to set higher aims. The situations you use to tolerate are no longer acceptable. Determine the specific habits and behaviors you will need to practice every day to become the woman you want to become. These could be habits of determination, focus, persistence, patience, and working smart.

> **"When I dare to be powerful — to use my strength in the service of my vision, then it becomes less and less important whether I am afraid." Audre Lorde**

Are You Committed?

Exercise: **Explain your new mindset on your commitment to your goals.** Write it out, post it all around your home, put it in your car, and tape it on your bathroom mirrors. Say it to yourself while you are looking directly into the mirror face to face with yourself. It may feel uncomfortable at first, but you now know that staying within a comfort zone will keep you broke and unfulfilled.

_____
_____
_____
_____
_____
_____
_____
_____

Key points:

- Be committed to your vision regardless of the circumstances.
- Great success does not come easy.
- Be flexible in pursuit of your goals.
- Take responsibility for your results.

CHAPTER VIII
CREATING YOUR CIRCLE OF TRUST

CHAPTER VIII
CREATING YOUR CIRCLE OF TRUST

> "Build relationships with people who can help you grow, but don't be selfish. You must bring something to the table as well." Deborah Francis

In life, if you want to be successful, you need a team of like-minded individuals who are not afraid to hold you accountable. Each of us has groups of people with whom we surround ourselves. We have our business associates, we have our friends, and we have our family members. Many times, these people have a much greater influence on us than we might think. Many people do not achieve the success they desire because of the people they have allowed in their circle.

The individuals we allow in our circle can either propel us toward success or they can be a hindrance. To succeed in creating a prosperous life, you have to surround yourself with people who believe in your success and want you to succeed. Your inner circle needs to be part of your success. My mentor advised me to choose my friends and business partners wisely. To be honest, I did not listen at first because I thought I knew who my real friends were; little did I know, I was in for a surprise.

When I started my first company, I thought all of my friends would be happy for my success and come support my endeavors. Some of the people I thought would be with me through thick and thin, in the end, became the people who were not happy for my success. Someone once told me that if you want to see who your true friends are, become successful or have a financial hardship.

Everyone is not going to applaud your success. This can be difficult for women who are not emotionally strong, or those who value other people's opinion above their own.

> "No matter what accomplishments you make, somebody helped you." Althea Gibson

Having the right people around you is critical to your success. To pursue success effectively, you must build supportive relationships that will help you work toward your goals. No one ever achieved success on his or her own. It is not wise to try and do it by yourself. Everyone needs some sort of help; Jesus recruited 12 disciples to help spread the message. You can achieve infinitely more with strategic partners than you ever could by yourself. **Partnering is the key to removing your limited resources. It multiplies your own potential.**

Building Relationships

To build those relationships, you need to learn to trust others and they must trust you in turn. No person has ever possessed enough resources—when I say resources, I am referring to time, talent and money—to achieve extraordinary success on their own. We all need a team. Every woman who has ever achieved extraordinary success, whether personally or professionally, has done it with a great deal of help from others. When you understand that you do not have all the necessary resources to achieve your dreams, it forces you to look for mentors who are rich in knowledge and resources. You may have the talent or ideas for a new business venture, but you may lack the time or the money to effectively pursue this business venture. In this case, you can partner with someone who may have the time and also partner with someone who may have the money for investment capital. **You can get more done with a team than you can on your own.**

Warning: There will always be those who say that something cannot be done or worse, that you cannot do it. Someone once told me that there are only a few negative people in the world and they just travel around, more frequently ending up wherever you are. To fulfill your desires, it will require an unwavering commitment to your goals that cannot be shaken by the negative, often uneducated and misinformed, comments of others. You must, at all cost, watch who you allow into your trusted circle. Many people may become a distraction and you will have to limit your time with them as you travel on your journey.

Relationship is about giving, not getting. This is where I think most people make the biggest mistake in their relationships. People are always looking at what they are getting out of the relationship instead of what they are giving to it. If you go into relationships wanting to get rather than give, you will always lose. No relationship will work well if either party does not do what they promise to do.

The best relationships that survive and succeed are those when each person takes responsibility and follows through on their commitment. Building good quality relationships takes time and is something that you constantly have to work at if you want the relationship to be meaningful. Relationships do not just happen; you need to learn to understand people and their basic wants and desires in order to have great relationships. You should know how to deal with people and understand that all the same rules apply whether you are close to the person or not.

If you are having trouble building quality relationships, I highly recommend you read Dale Carnegie's *How to Win Friends and Influence People*. This book has done wonders for me and my business. I actually read this book once a year because I have learned that to have quality relationships, I must continue to learn what it takes to sustain these relationships. For example, my husband knows I love him. Yes, he should know this but if I do not show my love by encouraging him or believing in his business ideas, it will definitely have an effect on my marriage and not in a positive way.

The same goes with my children; they are a part of my inner circle. I need to remember to compliment them. They know I love them; I have been feeding them and caring after their needs for all these years. I value my relationship with my family, friends, and my business partners, so I must continue to grow—not just for them but for me. Your relationships will always mirror back to you exactly the kind of person you are. When you are happy and optimistic and at peace, your relationships will be happy and harmonious and loving. But when your thinking is disrupted or negative for any reason, consciously or unconsciously, this will be immediately reflected in your relationships.

When you develop your circle of trust, select members who would hold you accountable and not allow you to slack off from your commitments. **Select leaders who do not give less than their best**. Make sure they take pride in being in your circle; only accept standards of excellence and never allow anyone to corrupt these standards.

If you associate with negative people, you tend to become negative. If you keep company with a con artist or a thief, people will soon begin to associate you with these attributes. The proverb states, "birds of a feather flock together." Start spending time with people who are moving toward success. Look for people who are goal-oriented, motivated and career-minded.

Mastermind Groups

Remember: success leaves clues, so the most effective way to achieve success is to associate with other successful people. If you want to be relentless, associate with relentless people. If want to be wealthy, associate with wealthy people to develop prosperous ideas. Choosing your associates is important because over the course of time, people become like the people with whom they associate. If you surround yourself with positive-thinking people, you will begin to see the benefits of positive thinking working in your life. As you begin to make the necessary changes and commitment to prospering and being successful, you are going to have to build a team. Author Napoleon Hill called this having a "mastermind" group.

I sought out wealthy people who achieved success and were willing to share their principles with me so I could achieve what I wanted in life. To my surprise, there were many successful people who were willing to take the time to mentor me. They saw the fire in my eyes and I was serious about achieving my goals. I truly valued their time, so I made the most of it. **Key: If someone is willing to spend time with you and mentor you, make sure you respect their time.**

Comparison

Do you constantly compare yourself to others? Comparing ourselves to others does more harm to a relationship than good. No one likes to be around a woman who is always trying to one up them. You remodel your kitchen and they go and buy a new house. You have finger food at your party and they go and hire a personal chef for their party. Comparison does not motivate you to do better; instead, it makes you feel like you will never be good enough. When women compare themselves in an attempt to measure their own success, they set themselves up for nothing more than mediocrity. **Using others as your yardstick places a limit on your success**. Most women do not need to worry about other women being in competition with them. Other women are not the reason that they fail at achieving their life goals. Rather, they disqualify themselves with a lack of discipline, direction, and focus.

Success

Women who have a fear of success tend to separate themselves from other women who are successful, because those who dare to risk and achieve remind them of what they are not doing. To avoid this pain, they usually condemn those who are successful. Only when you are able to truly appreciate and enjoy the success of others are you setting up the right mental attitude to be successful yourself. Each time we sincerely applaud others for their achievements, we can rest assured our own success is coming closer because our consciousness is focused on success.

Few people dare to compare themselves to the those who are successful and those who do, usually look to successful people as a source of inspiration. People who lack self-confidence can find it difficult to become successful.

Many people lack self-confidence and are unwilling to set their aims higher for fear of failing. This can sometimes stem from the people who are discouraging them because they feel their goals and life choices are unrealistic. It may be that friends and family do not approve, so they use ridicule to prevent their loved one from making what they feel like is a mistake.

If you read the autobiographies or biographies of some of the world's most successful people, you will see they did not let their circumstances or environment determine their outcome. Our success, or lack of it, can be influenced by the people with whom we associate. If you associate with people who are successful or determined to be successful, you will pattern your actions accordingly.

If you aspire to be successful in life, you must be able to build and maintain meaningful relationships. You must become someone who is able to inspire and develop others, a person of loyalty, respect, and trust. Most importantly, you must choose your relationships wisely. As you consider your definition of prosperity, remember that your success will ultimately be based on the quality of relationships you develop with other successful people.

Do whatever it takes to create relationships with people who will hold you accountable and help you keep your commitments.

Create relationships with people who will hold you accountable and encourage you on the path to your goals. Find ways to spend more time with people who love to help and build up others to their fullest potential. Only share your vision with people who will support you, not those who will respond with cynicism or indifference.

If you want to start a business, for instance, subscribe to business magazines and start befriending those who already have successful businesses. You will find that their attitude is infectious and you will start believing that you can be successful in business, too. Being around people who have created successful businesses can be extremely motivating. A great place to meet other business owners is through your local chamber of commerce or a trade association.

Write 10 qualities you value in a relationship. *Focus on what you want in a relationship, not on what you do not want.*

1. _____

2. _____

3. _____

4. _____

5. _____

6. _____

7. _____

8. _____

9. _____

10. _____

Do You Have a Mentor?

Make a list of five individuals who you would consider or would like to mentor you for each area of life. It can be someone from your local community or someone you admire.

Leadership Mentors

1. _____
2. _____
3. _____
4. _____
5. _____

Spiritual Mentors

1. _____
2. _____
3. _____
4. _____
5. _____

Family Mentors

1._____

2._____

3._____

4._____

5._____

Health Mentors

1._____

2._____

3._____

4._____

5._____

Financial Mentors

1. _____

2. _____

3. _____

4. _____

5. _____

Relationship Mentors

1. _____

2. _____

3. _____

4. _____

5. _____

Business Mentors

1._____

2._____

3._____

4._____

5._____

Having mentors is important to your success. Many have already traveled the road you may be on. I remember the words from my mentor, "Always learn from other people's mistakes and success. It will save you time and money." Through my experience in life, I have seen people who have dreamed big dreams but failed to live them out due to the people they surrounded themselves with. I learned early that everyone is not going to arrive at the same destination with you. The people who may have started with you may not be the same ones who finish with you.

There is going to be some new faces and places as you grow and develop. Although this can be difficult for some people, you also need to remove the negative people from your life. My mentor said he could see my future just by looking at the five people with whom I spend the most time.

To be honest, I did not like what I saw. I had to change my circle of friends. It was not that they were bad people, we were just headed in two different directions in life. My desire was to be a business owner and not live from paycheck to paycheck. I wanted to travel and meet new people. It was when I started to change my associations and got around people who wanted or had successful businesses that my thinking began to expand.

Once your thinking expands, it is difficult to do things the same. One of the reasons people fail to start their own businesses, for instance, is that they spend most of their time associating with people who do not even have a personal vision for their life. **Mindsets are contagious, so spend your time with people whose mindset is worth catching.**

Key points:

- Build relationships with people who can help and will encourage you as you achieve goals.

- Spend more time with other successful people. Mindsets are contagious.

- Everyone is not going to be happy for your success. Separate from those who do not believe in your vision.

- Find mentors who achieved what you desire and ask to be mentored by them.

- Applaud other people's success.

CHAPTER IX
I SHALL HAVE WHAT I DESIRE

CHAPTER IX
I SHALL HAVE WHAT I DESIRE

> "Burning desire to be or do something gives us staying power - a reason to get up every morning or to pick ourselves up and start in again after a disappointment."
> Marsha Sinetar

In the previous chapters of this book, we focused on your thoughts, beliefs, attitudes, vision, decisions, commitment and your circle of trust. These are the key components in building a prosperous life, but it takes a burning desire to bring manifestation of prosperity into your life.

Your desire must be stronger than your circumstances. When my business partners and I first built our investment business, we were strapped for cash in the beginning stages as a company. Any cash flow we received, we reinvested it back into the business and we knew that all the sacrifices we made were going to pay off. Some of the executives, including myself, did not take a salary for the first two years.

Our desire for building a successful company was much greater than our short-term cash flow circumstances. We knew what we wanted, we created the vision, we developed the plan, and we took action. All these things are fine and well but if we did not have the desire that was strong enough to get us through the rough periods, we would have given up in the earlier stages.

So I understand and know what it is like to face unfavorable circumstances in business and in life. You know, I would not trade any of those situations for anything.

The tough times made me stronger and gave me something that could not be bought or sold: an unquenchable desire to see my dreams and goals come to pass. My mentor expressed to me, "When you make the decision to be successful, just be prepared for a butt kicking." These were not the exact words; I have to keep it PG for the mature audience.

Got Desire?

Desire is like gas in the engine, and what good is a car without gas? Without the gas, you will be stuck in the garage or you will break down on the side of the road. It will be the same in life if you do not have the desire to achieve your goals. No lukewarm effort or indifferent ambition ever accomplished anything. Many people make halfhearted effort in life, their resolutions are spineless, there is no backbone in their endeavor, and no grit in their ambition. Desire is a powerful force of attraction that acts like a magnet drawing toward us that which we desire.

People who live ordinary, mundane lives have not gotten in touch with their true desires. At some point in life, they just gave up or stopped dreaming all together. In order to achieve great things in life, have extraordinary relationships, or a healthy body, you must have a burning desire. Oh, yes, if you want a healthy body, you must have the desire to do what is necessary to develop and maintain it.

Whatever we long for, struggle for, and hold persistently in the mind, we tend to become in exact proportion to the intensity and persistency of the thought. **Life gives us exactly what we desire—nothing more, nothing less**. You are now only what you desire to be. By every thought and every feeling growing out of your mind, you have created the environment in which you now live.

Whether the environment is prosperous or lacking, large or small, successful or failing, you and you alone are responsible. If you want to achieve great things in life, you must decide definitely where you want to be.

The purpose of life is to enjoy it and live it to the fullest. Life is too short to waste doing anything you do not enjoy. Dorothea Brande stated in her best-selling book *Wake up and live*, "All that is necessary to break the spell of inertia and frustration is this: Act as if it were impossible to fail." There is a huge difference between living a positive productive life and barely existing or surviving. How and why we live is much more important than simply living. **It should come as no surprise that more often than not, the people who end up being successful in life are the ones who know exactly what they want; they take the time to write down their goals and they focus on their desires, while taking action daily to achieve their goals.**

What do you desire in life?

When you write your goals, you are putting them in visible form. Until you actually write your goals, it was just sort of this notion in your mind. Once written you can now see it, you can read them over and make adjustments where needed. And not only that, you can review your goals on a regular basis. It would be most helpful to write your goals on an index card keep it with you and look at it at least four times a day. The reason behind this method is, the more you visualize and know exactly what it is you desire, you tend to move toward those things in life.

> "It is for us to pray not for tasks equal to our power, but for power equal to our task, to go forward with a great desire forever beating at the door of our hearts as we travel toward our distant goal." Helen Keller

People with goals know exactly where they are going. Goal-oriented people make up their mind about exactly what they want and keep their eyes and enthusiasm on that goal until it becomes a reality in their lives. Be intentional about setting and achieving your goals. Do this every day and it will become a habit that will lead you continuously toward them. These goals must be consistent with your values; we discussed this in the previous chapter. Your goals have to be consistent with what you believe to be true, valuable, and important. Success and true happiness is when your desires are in line with your life values and purpose.

You must always evaluate what it is you truly desire in life because sometimes your desires may lead you away from your values if you are not mindful of them.

One of the most common complaints I have heard from people over the years is that in the pursuit of their goals, their life became unbalanced. They spent too much time focusing on one or two areas of their life and not enough in others. While in pursuit of reaching the top in their careers, they may have neglected their health or neglected spending quality time with their loved ones. This can happen to anyone who does not take the time to evaluate their priorities in life. **Remember that life will give you what you truly desire, but make sure you have someone to share it with.**

> "The sharing of joy, whether physical, emotional, psychic, or intellectual, forms a bridge between the sharers which can be the basis for understanding much of what is not shared between them, and lessens the threat of their difference."
> Audre Lorde

Success in life will not be handed to you; you must challenge your limiting beliefs and take massive action toward your goals. There is nothing in life that can defeat you or deny you of success but yourself. No conditions can overtake you if you set life goals and focus consistently and persistently on your goals. Your own limiting thinking can defeat you, your lack of determination, indecisiveness, and lack of confidence in yourself can defeat you. Your success in life is up to you. **"According to thy faith be it unto thee." Matthew 9:29**

Most people who continuously fail to achieve what they desire in life is because of their lack of faith in themselves. In the pursuit of their goals they did not believe enough in themselves, they focused too much on their life circumstances and they gave up. Most are not willing to pay the price for what they desire, when they are faced with opposition or when they get knocked down, they do not have the courage to get back up and go at it again. The instant you acknowledge that you are incapable of doing the thing you set out to do, or that some outside circumstances can block you from achieving your desires, you set up a barrier to your success that no amount of hard work can remove. Nothing is more detrimental to success than this sort of mental attitude.

We get in this life whatever we concentrate upon with our mind. Our success or failure is in our own hands. Prosperous women have prosperous attitudes. They are convinced that they can accomplish what they set out to accomplish, and that there is no reason why they cannot achieve all that they desire. Prosperous women expect more good out of life; they expect to succeed without compromising their core values. Women with the best attitude naturally rise to the top. **Think about what you desire, talk it, live it, breathe it, dream it, act it, and saturate your life with it. You must believe that what you desire is already yours.**

Where will you be in your life five years from today?

If you have completed the exercise, I commend you for taking part in your success and also being coachable. You have to realize that you live in a world where you are the architect of your future; therefore, you create what happens. You have got to accept 100% responsibility for where you are, who you are with, and what is happening to you.

You have got to decide what sort of life you want to lead. A success consciousness is a self-fulfilling reality. The more you start to think success, the more it will start to happen for you; the more you start to believe in it, the more you will be excited by it; the more your mind will get even more creative to come up with the next great idea; and the more you will go out there to find some new creative ways of doing things.

Key points:

- We get in this life whatever we concentrate upon with all of our mind.
- Success in life will not be handed to you.
- People with goals know exactly where they are going.
- You have got to decide what sort of life you want to lead.
- You are the architect of your future.

CHAPTER X
WHAT TO DO NOW? TAKE ACTION!

CHAPTER X
WHAT TO DO NOW? TAKE ACTION

> "Stop putting energy into things that distract you from what really matters and what needs to get done. Strive to be consistent and relentless about being productive." Deborah Francis

Did you think I was going to leave you all puffed up, feeling good with no action? Absolutely not. This is not that type of book; it is time to get to work. By reading this book and doing the exercises in each of the chapters, you should have an understanding of the principles of creating a prosperous life; if not, read this book again. **As a matter of fact, read this book every three months; it will serve you well. Make sure you schedule it in your calendar. Commit and Take Action!**

Have you heard the saying that knowledge is power? Well it is not. **Applied knowledge is power.** Changing your life begins with information but after that, it is all about what you do with that information that will change and improve your life. Having knowledge means being able to make choices. The only way to create change is to take action. I like this quote by Oprah Winfrey: **"Think like a queen. A queen is not afraid to fail. Failure is another steppingstone to greatness."**

Once you set a goal for yourself, you must act immediately; without action, you cannot expect to achieve anything different in your life. Too often, people get stuck in the state of "analysis paralysis" and never reach the action stage. They have to have a meeting and then have a meeting about the meeting. You can create plans all day, but get moving. **Just identify the first physical action you need to take and then do it.** For instance, if you have decided to have a better relationship with your spouse, go on a date and turn off the television. **Do not think about it, do not ponder it, just do it!**

The time has come to go out and achieve your goals and live a life of prosperity. We have discussed the importance of your thoughts, words, attitude and your belief in building a life you desire. **You have made the decision and I know you are committed to the process; you have come too far to turn back now.**

One of the principles of success is recognizing that a burning desire follows action. The momentum of continuous action fuels the desire, while procrastination kills the desire. So **act boldly** as if it is impossible to fail. If you keep adding fuel to your desire, you will reach the point of knowing that you will never quit, and ultimate success will be achieved in a matter of time.

> "The future belongs to those who believe in the beauty of their dreams." Eleanor Roosevelt

There are so many people who want to change or want more out of life than they are getting, but they are not willing to take action in getting what they want. It is fine to talk about what you want and even to dream about what you want but if you are not taking action, you will become frustrated in life.

Plans and no action will keep you in the same position you are in. Many people make plans but they do not take the time to put those plans into action. Their favorite words are, "I'm trying to." **The mindset of those who go out and achieve their goals is either I do or I don't; there is no such thing as trying.** I would rather watch a leader than listen to one. **Action is the key.**

Whatever desire you may have, it will only be fulfilled if action is taken. First, you must decide what it is you need to make yourself content with your life and give yourself step by step aims. You have to consider how much work you need to put in if you are ever to begin achieving those aims. Next, you should set a timeline for reaching your goals and then create a plan highlighting how and when you will go about your tasks.

In order to turn the wheel of your consciousness and to begin to walk in prosperity, you must do things you have never done before. As a leader, parent, business owner, or whatever is your current circumstances in life, it is your responsibility to change your conditions. You have the power to do it. **Does your vision inspire you enough to take action?**

To assist you on this journey, we will provide you with some action steps to take. Use the action steps as a building block and once you develop the proper habits, create an action plan that works best for you. **You have to do what works for you.** We will be your coach and guide until you come into your own.

We are going to create some action steps for each area of your life. These steps are foundational for creating a prosperous life but they will only work wonders for you if you **take action** and do them. Remember, all that you need is already on the inside of you. **Your life begins to become great only when you decide upon your major definite purpose and then work on it every single day**. The first area we are going to focus on is the spiritual area of life. This is the foundation and key for developing your life.

Spiritual Development: Got Faith?

> "The spiritual path - is simply the journey of living our lives. Everyone is on a spiritual path; most people just don't know it." Marianne Williamson

Before we begin, let me make this clear: **Your relationship with God is personal and it is between You and God.** So you must take this area of development in your life seriously.

Spending time with God opens a realm in which He shares wisdom, knowledge and understanding with you about circumstances you may be facing. In order to know God as the Creator, you must spend time with Him daily. God desires the best for our life, so we must make time for God in our daily activities. How you spend time and connect with God is up to you; this is your *personal* relationship with God.

I found this to be the most important area of **my life**. I took notice of this when I began studying the Bible for myself. At first, I thought the Bible was a book filled with do's and don'ts: don't eat this, don't go there, don't say that, and love thy enemy (wow, that was a hard one). I truly believe the reason I thought this way was because I had someone else's opinion about what and who God is. In my earlier years, I never took the time to study the Word of God for myself. I always relied on someone else's interpretation of God's Word. I began to have some understanding when I came across this passage in **1 John 4:8: He that loveth not knoweth not God; for God is love.**

Once I found out that God is love, the next thing I had to do was seek what is true about **Love**. And I found it in another passage; we actually used the passage in our wedding and it has been our foundation scripture for our marriage: **1 Corinthians 13:4-8 (NIV): Love is patient, love is kind. It does not envy, it does not boast, it is not proud. It does not dishonor others, it is not self-seeking, it is not easily angered, it keeps no record of wrongs. Love does not**

delight in evil but rejoices with the truth. It always protects, always trusts, always hopes, and always perseveres. Love never fails.

I really like **"Love never fails."** And you know what, since I began seeking God, He has never failed me. Did I have some circumstances I did not think was fair? Yes, but I learned to look at things that are unfavorable as learning experiences. I believe in all the adversity I faced in life, God was shaping and molding me into a greater woman. **Isaiah 64:8: But now, O LORD, thou art our father; we are the clay, and thou our potter; and we all are the work of thy hand**. It took time for me to understand this; it was a spiritual process. **Spiritual principles can only be discerned spiritually.**

Spiritual growth is a process of shedding our wrong and unreal conceptions, thoughts, beliefs and ideas, and becoming more and more conscious and aware of the God within us. French philosopher Teilhard de Chardin stated, **"We are not human beings having a spiritual experience. We are spiritual beings having a human experience."**

Having an understanding of our spiritual nature is of great importance for everyone, not only for people who seek a deeper connection to God or attend a religious service. Spiritual growth is the basis for a better and more harmonious life for everyone—a life free of tension, fear and anxiety.

Spiritual growth is not a means for escaping from responsibilities, behaving strangely and becoming an impractical woman. It is a method of growing and becoming a stronger, happier and more responsible woman. A balanced life requires that you take care not only of the necessities of the body, feelings and mind, but also of the spirit; and this is the role of spiritual growth.

Spiritual Action Steps:

- If you have a library card, check out an uplifting spiritual book. The book you choose is up to you. Take some time each morning to seek and find the meaning of having a relationship with God.

- Be grateful for what you currently have in your life. Write five things you are grateful for each night before you go to bed. Gratitude draws you closer to God.

- Learn to quiet your mind through prayer, concentration exercises, and meditation. Focus on what is on the inside of you and try to find out what is it that makes you feel alive.

Personal Development: Got a Growth Plan?

> "If you don't like something, change it. If you can't change it, change your attitude!" Maya Angelou

The next area we are going to focus on is personal development. Success is an on-going process. Development does not stop after this book; this is just the beginning. There is so much more to learn; you must be a life-long learner. Development takes time and involves a range of experiences, guidance and training. **Your goal is to develop the skills that support the competencies needed to succeed in life**.

Having a personal development plan is a wise investment in yourself. The reason it is called personal development is because the plan is personal to you. When you make your own personal development plan, it can provide you with a self-reflection. One of the objectives of this endeavor is the assessment of your capabilities, including your skills, personal strengths, and knowledge. You can develop a plan that focuses on your areas of strengths or weaknesses.

When I started the process of developing myself, I became amazed at all the information and resources that were available. All the solutions to life circumstances were in books; all I had to do was find the book and apply the principles to get the results I desired. The problem was in the "**consistent applying of the principles**." I would read book after book and not see any results. I would hear someone say a certain book changed their life and I would run out and get that book. I was addicted to the personal development process. My growth plan was not focused. At first, I never took the time out to apply the principles in many of these books, I was reading just to say I read a personal growth book.

Then something happened. I was at an event and heard several speakers, who were successful businessmen and women, say Napoleon Hill's *Think and Grow Rich* helped change their life. That was not my first time hearing someone say that book changed their life. At that point, I had already read *Think and Grow Rich* and I was not at the point of wealth that I desired to be as yet.

I got to a point in my life where I decided enough is enough. I will no longer play the victim or continue down the path of missed opportunities. I got tired of my life going around and around in circles, only to end up with the same results. I started to ask myself: "Why are they successful? What do they have that I do not have? And why is my life like this? What do I need to do to get better results?" **I wanted more, so I began my journey on being a great student of life, so I could be an outstanding teacher of living.**

In life, you must plan for personal development. The first step is to make a true analysis of "Where am I today?" and "Where do I want to go?" Second, you must identify resources available to help you get there. Third, you must implement a plan that can lead to successful development. Of all the successful people I know, they have made it a habit of creating a development plan.

Actions Steps for Personal Development:

- Apply for a library card; it's free. If you have one, great. The library is going to become your second home. **Be a lifelong learner.**

- Go to the library and check out one of the books we have in the recommended reading list in the back of this book. Select one that you may be interested in. Most importantly, **pick the book up and read it.**

- **Turn your vehicle into Drive Time University.** Instead of being bombarded with advertising and constant negative news, listen to audio programs that inspire you. Some of the books in the recommended reading list are in audio format as well.

- Take a break from the television for a week. This may be difficult if you are addicted and I hope it is difficult for you to do; **I want you to be uncomfortable.** Living in the comfort zone is a sure fire way to ensure your own misery.

- Create a personal journal. Write your thoughts. Record big and small successes, your techniques for beating difficulties and your achievements.

You will be creating your blueprint for success.

Health Plan: Did You Eat Your Broccoli?

> "Women in particular need to keep an eye on their physical and mental health, because if we're scurrying to and from appointments and errands, we don't have a lot of time to take care of ourselves. We need to do a better job of putting ourselves higher on our own 'to do' list." Michelle Obama

What is the point of wealth without health? My motto is: "Without health, you will not enjoy your wealth." What purpose is there to have all the wealth you desire but not the health to enjoy it? Taking control of your health is of utmost importance, because your body and mind are your most valuable assets which determine your well-being. You can create a healthy lifestyle by making conscious choices. The components of healthy living also include practicing healthy habits like exercising and clean-eating. Taking control of your health will result in more energy, mental alertness, enthusiasm, and creativity.

Getting the proper and adequate nutrition is important. Your body requires fresh food and plenty of water. Fresh fruits and vegetables provide nutrients and enzymes. A healthy diet can lead to better overall performance of the mind and body. According to the U.S. Department of Agriculture, foods high in antioxidants can help promote improved cognitive functioning. Our diet plays an important role in our mood and mental health. According to the *American Journal of Psychiatry*, a healthy diet is associated with a lower incidence of depression, anxiety disorders and dysthymia, compared to a typical "Western" diet high in sugar, processed foods and alcohol.

When we start eating healthy, we begin to get more dietary fiber into our systems and suddenly, our digestive systems begin to work better. When you eliminate high-fat meat and processed foods from your diet, then much of your body's energy is freed from the intense work of digesting these foods. Detoxification helps—your blood, your organs, and your brain become clearer. You begin to become more cognizant of the toxic nature of the food you have been consuming.

Toxicity entering the body is of much greater concern in the 20th century than ever before. There are many new and stronger chemicals, air and water pollution, radiation and atomic power. We ingest chemicals, utilize more drugs of all kinds, eat more sugar and refined foods, and daily abuse ourselves with assorted stimulants and sedatives. The incidence of a lot of toxic diseases has also increased; cancer and cardiovascular disease are two of the main ones. Arthritis, allergies, obesity and many skin problems are others.

Additionally, a wide range of symptoms like headaches, tiredness, pains, coughs, gastrointestinal problems, and issues from immune weakness may all be related to toxicity. When you begin a plant-based eating plan, your body finally cleanses itself of the noxious effects of these toxic foods and substances

Health Action Steps:

- **Drink more water.** Develop the habit of drinking more water than flavored drinks. Drink at least half your body weight in ounces of water per day.

- **Exercise for 20 minutes daily.** It can be walking, running, or weight lifting or an exercise you enjoy. Be consistent.

- **Eat more fruits and vegetables.** Eating healthy is important. There are some great nutrition books, check out, **The Joy of Healthy Living:** The Guide for Eating Right for Life

- **Take time to relax.** Take 20 minutes daily for yourself where you can focus on breathing and calming all the noise in your mind.

- **Get rest, get rest, get rest.** Give your body the proper rest it needs. Believe me, I know what can be done to a body that has not received proper rest.

- **Give your body the essentials it needs for healthy living with whole food supplements**. Make sure you research the company and the product before you use the product. **Check out Juice Plus:** http://Deborah.JuicePlus.com/

Relationship-Building: Who's In Your Network?

> "I can trust my friends... These people force me to examine myself, encourage me to grow." Cher

A strong, healthy relationship can be one of the best supports in your life. Good relationships improve your life in all aspects, strengthening your health, mind, and connection with others. However, it can also be one of the greatest drains if the relationship is not working. **Relationships are an investment. The more you put in, the more you get back**. Love and relationships take work, commitment, and a willingness to adapt and change through life as a team.

It is important that you develop the right relationships. When most people talk about relationships, they usually say they want a 50-50 relationship. Why would you want to give only half of your potential? **For a relationship to be meaningful, you must give 100%.**

Important Ingredients of a Relationship

Communication is at the top of the list for relationship building; yet we are rarely taught how to communicate effectively. My mentor once shared with me an insight that I am forever grateful for: "God gave us one mouth and two ears for a reason. We need to learn how to talk less and listen more." Have you noticed that when you are with people who are great listeners, they seem to have a magnetism about them? You just seem to be drawn to them. On the other hand, when you are in the presence of an infamous talker, you feel mentally drained afterwards.

In a relationship, communication is about sharing, which consists of each person being able to express himself or herself freely without the opposite party placing judgment. When you know how to give and receive, you can develop some wonderful lifelong relationships. You could have all the money in the world but if you do not have someone special to share it with, it would be senseless. Life could be lonely without good people to experience it with.

I just realized something: Benjamin Franklin, Andrew Jackson, Abraham Lincoln or George Washington ($$$money$$$) never hugged me in the middle of the night. It would be scary if they did, but you know what I mean.

- **Quality Relationships + Money = Wonderful Experiences**

- **Money – Quality Relationships = Lonely Life**

- **Quality Relationships – Money = Donation-Based Life**

"The poor is hated even of his own neighbour: but the rich hath many friends." **Proverbs 14:20**

"Wealth maketh many friends; but the poor is separated from his neighbour." **Proverbs 19:4**

So how do you build quality relationships? First, you must set the example. **"A true friend sees the first tear… catches the second… and stops the third."** If you do not know what it means to be a friend, in Chapter VIII, we did an exercise listing the 10 qualities you value in a relationship. Take those qualities and exemplify them. Next, you must respect others. In order to get respect, you must first show respect.

A major stumbling block in any relationship is the proper way to settling disagreements. When you are wrong, learn to admit your mistakes. This could be a hard one, because we live in a world where everyone wants to be right. If we learn to communicate effectively with others and are willing to share our true feelings and respect other people's feelings, many benefits will await us as we learn to build relationships with one another.

Relationships Action Steps:

- Make a list of all the successful people you personally know who have great relationships, and take each one of them to lunch individually. Ask them questions about how they developed their relationships. Make this a lunch and learn.

- Attend one networking event each month. Make a new contact while you are there.

- Treat everyone you meet with respect no matter who they are.

- Learn to be a great listener.

Business/Career Development: Mind Your Business

> "A mediocre idea that generates enthusiasm will go further than a great idea that inspires no one." Mary Kay Ash

In this area, we are going to focus on developing and maintaining a business. You may be thinking, "I don't want to be a business owner; I would rather work for someone." The truth is, even if you get a job or build a career, you would still need to treat it as a business. Some of the principles we discuss in this section could be applied to a career as well. It takes courage and commitment to be a business owner, but there are benefits and risks in owning a business.

Let's look at some of the positives of entrepreneurship:

You have control over your salary. You determine how much you are worth.

- You control your time. You decide how many hours you are going to work.

- You are in charge of your own destiny. You make the decisions; no one can tell you when you can go to the bathroom or on vacation. You can promote yourself anytime.

- You have options. You can decide how many employees you want to hire.

- You can become a community builder. Your business can have a positive effect on the community.

Now, are you ready to start your business? Here are some of the most important questions you must ask before you journey into entrepreneurship:

Will my product or service add value to the market? Let's be honest: the startup phase in a business is time-consuming. You will find yourself questioning whether you have made the right decision, especially when the hours are long and the initial profits (if any) are lean. Starting a company from the ground up is no get-rich-quick thing. As the business owner, you are also the number one salesperson for your organization. Your enthusiasm for your product or service—whether it is health products or international business consulting—is often the difference that brings purchasing customers, lands deals, and attracts investors. It is unwise to start down the path of entrepreneurship unless you have a zeal that will get you through rough patches and keep you interested long after the initial enthusiasm has faded.

Do I have a business plan? A business plan provides an outline of the vision, overview, and goals of your new business. It will help you stay on track while you build your business; and referring back to this plan will redirect focus to your original intentions for creating the business. This plan is not only for you to view, but also for investors who will evaluate your business strategy.

What is my IQ (I Quit) level? Whether it is resigning from your day job or opening a storefront office, nothing about starting a business is for the faint of heart. This is not for the employee-minded or those looking for a steady paycheck. **"Take action, and be willing to jump off the cliff and figure out how to fly on the way down."** There is no guarantee of success or even a steady paycheck. If you are risk-averse, entrepreneurship is probably not the right path for you. Stick with your day job.

Am I an effective decision maker? No one else is going to make decisions for you when you own your own business. You cannot call mommy. **Consider how you might handle these early decisions:** Do I incorporate? Do I use a corporate tax ID or my social security number? Do I use my hard earned savings or get a loan? Do I work from home or do I purchase office space? Do I hire employees? How much do I invest in marketing? Keep in mind that the decision-making process only gets more complicated as time goes on once you have employees or clients depending on you. The choices you make can lead to success or failure, so you must feel confident in your ability to make the right call.

Am I willing to be the CEO, manager, and janitor? While a corporate employee focuses on a special skill or role within the larger company, a business owner must contribute everything to the business. Startup entrepreneurs in particular must be versatile and play a number of roles from chief salesperson to bookkeeper to head marketer and bill collector. If juggling many roles does not suit you, entrepreneurship probably will not either.

Am I willing to go the distance? Working six days a week instead of a 9-to-5 schedule, abandoning old hobbies and interests, and not spending quality time with your loved ones can quickly lead to doubts and fears in the midst of a business's initial startup. If you do not have the discipline and focus, the beginning stages of building your business can lead to failure. This is what happens to many first-time entrepreneurs. If you are able to develop and maintain good habits that create a balance between your life and your business—such as not working on certain days, making time for hobbies such as reading, exercising, and going on weekly dates with your spouse—life as an entrepreneur can be rewarding and most importantly, fun.

Cash flow is one of the key elements to taking your business to the next level. A business that does earn and manage its revenue can cause a great deal of stress to first-time business owners. With most startups, it may take some time before the business beings to generate cash flow, and that is okay. But you must determine how much time you are willing to invest in a business that is not generating cash flow. Is your team willing to stick and stay? If you are interested in laying a foundation for a profitable business currently and into the future, you must inspect what you expect. Put it all in writing so you can have it before you. If you need help analyzing the numbers, seek professional counsel from someone who has experience in running a successful business. The objective for your business is to track your income and expenses so that you put your business in a position to prosper. And you do want to prosper, correct?

Excuse me, business owner: Got cash flow? Proper management of the cash flow in your business will determine the long-term success of your company. A business that has no cash flow is considered a hobby, and we all know hobbies cost money. If you are a business owner and there is a cash flow issue, you will need to do a complete analysis of your business model from the top down.

Do you have a blueprint for success for your business? Got cash?
Cash is king in business. When cash is flowing in a business, it gives the business an opportunity for expansion such as hiring new team members to take the business to the next level, or maybe expanding the business to an international market. Many first-time business owners fail at properly managing cash flow. Instead of reinvesting back into their business, they take the cash and spend it on personal use. I have seen this happen many times with people who make that transition from being an employee to an entrepreneur. They are so use to having a paycheck coming in on a consistent basis that when their business starts to earn revenue, they eat the first fruits from the tree instead of planting the seeds to grow a bigger tree.

Cash flow management is essential for a business to succeed.

You must realize that your business is an asset that will thrive when you analyze where your business is currently and then move into the mode of creating cash flow projection. Savvy business owners know how to create and come within the constraints of a cash flow analysis based on a weekly, monthly and yearly projection. When you have been in business for a few years, a review of your company's cash flow patterns will help you to evaluate any areas that need to be amplified so your business can continue to grow.

Business/Career

- Decide if you are going to be an employee or an entrepreneur. Then develop a roadmap for your job or business success.

- Find a mentor who is currently successful in a business or area you are looking to develop a career in and invite them out to lunch. You pay. **Lunch and learn!**

- Create a list of things you are good at and could potentially turn into a business. Research the internet and see if there are businesses like the one you want to produce.

- Seek the advice of leaders in your industry, business bankers, and business financial planners who have attained high levels of success and are willing to empower you to reach your goals.

Financial Plan: Cash or Credit?

> "Be a Rich Woman! Rich in spirit...Rich in family and friends...Rich life experiences." Kim Kiyosaki

You must take responsibility for your financial state. It is going to take money to live a prosperous life. Eating healthy is going to require money, having the experiences that support meaningful relationships requires money, starting a business requires money. Prosperity does not run on credit. **If you are going to operate in this world, you are going to need money.**

Most people think that earning a large six- or seven-figure income is the key to financial freedom, but it is not. I know many people who earn a six- or seven-figure income, but they spend every dime of it and end up spending more than they earn by trying to keep up with the Joneses. They smell good and look good, but they are broke. You know how I know this? Because I once lived in that world. Years ago when I started making some real money, I did not have the financial discipline or mindset to accompany the money. You could say I was really out of control. I took exotic trips, I dined at the most expensive restaurants, and I bought new shoes and clothes like I was crazy. Did I think about saving or putting any money aside for investing or for a rainy day? Oh, no, it wasn't raining; it was sunny outside every day when I had money. Did I make some mistakes? Absolutely.

I have learned that if you try to live up to other people's financial standards of what automobile you should drive, where you should live, and what you should wear, you could end up in a great deal of trouble. And I was in trouble. I over-leveraged myself with debt obligations. At one point, I owed everyone and their mother. I got sick and tired of living that way; I was trying to impress people with money I did not have. I had many sleepless nights because I knew I could do better financially and never really liked owing money to anyone. I felt my bad money habits were a flaw in my character. I was not the type of person to hide from my creditors. I heard about people doing this but I was not buying into it. I wanted to be responsible; they loaned me the money and as a responsible person, my goal was to pay it back no matter the circumstances. When the creditors would call, I would simply say, "I don't have the money at the time but as soon as I get it, you will get your money." And you know what, I got treated with respect. I took responsibility for the financial decisions I made. From that moment on, I began to postpone the pleasures of the moment such as buying things on credit and spending every dime. I focused on wealth building by learning what successful people were doing with their wealth. I also began reading financial journals. **You could say I studied myself out of a broke mentality into a wealth mentality**. I had plenty of help as well. Thank God for my mentors. They say, "When the student is ready, the teacher will appear."

Do I have any regrets about how I used my money in the past? Absolutely... Not; it was a learning experience. I would have never gained this insight if I had not gone through that experience. Now I am free and I do not allow other people's opinion of me to determine what I desire in life. You will never be able to take charge of your life or really be free to be who you want to be until you to learn to accept full responsibility for your life right now. **One of the most important things in life is having your financial house in order**.

When you talk to financially successful people, they know how much they are worth, how much they earn monthly and/or annual basis, how much they pay in taxes, and they know exactly how much they are putting away toward their family legacy. They are thoughtful regarding every aspect of their financial life. As a result, they are never broke. They always have money in the bank. They enjoy a far higher standard of living than the average person. Your goal is to join the financial elite by thinking and acting the way they do.

It is time to get your financial house in order. To do this, you will need to have a financial tracking sheet or book where you can list all of your outstanding debt, monthly expenses, and income.

Financial Action Steps:

- Get a financial journal. This will help you keep track of your daily, monthly, and yearly expenses.

- Track your weekly, biweekly, and monthly income.

- Gather all your bills and write what your monthly expenses are.

- If you have credit card debt or any other debt, know the interest rate you are paying.

- Find a financial professional who is "successful with their finances" and take them out to lunch; you pay. **Lunch and learn!**

Start now! Do not procrastinate. Without implementing any of the action steps that you have mapped out for yourself, this book simply becomes an exercise in reading. In order to gain the full benefits this valuable book has to offer, make the decision here and now that you will act upon the strategies. You will achieve the kind of results in your life that you never thought possible. I want to see you wealthy!

90-Day Action Plan:

Create a list of goals you would like to achieve in the next 90 days. Write your goals in the present tense as though 90 days have passed and each of them has already been attained. Use the words, "I am, I earn, I drive, I have, I achieved," etc. Whenever you use the word "I" with regard to yourself, you program your subconscious mind to go to work on your goal all day long.

Assignment:

Purchase a recorder if you do not have one. I want you to record yourself speaking positive affirmations to yourself and listen to them twice daily: when you first wake up and just before you go to sleep. Your voice is the most powerful voice to your subconscious mind. Feed your mind with words that strengthen you and move you to act with passion.

The mechanics that make affirmations powerful are repetition, emotions, persistence and belief. You must feel what it would be like when the desire you are affirming is fulfilled or your needs are met. Every time you have a need and it is met, a certain feeling is produced in you. You need to evoke that same feeling when you state your affirmation.

Personalize your affirmations. They must resonate with you and feel right for you. The stronger your connection with the affirmation, the deeper the impression it makes on your mind, and the sooner you will experience positive results.

Affirmations:

- I now claim my birthright to Prosperity.
- I walk by faith, not by sight.
- I am love, I give love and I am loved.
- I am a Queen. I walk in my God-given power.
- I am at peace with my body. It is perfect.
- I wear my confidence as well as I wear my makeup.
- I am not given a spirit of fear, but of love and of power and of a sound mind.
- I choose to treat my body with care.
- I choose to give generously.
- I am open and willing, so I receive joyously.
- I am a strong woman.
- I am thankful and content today.
- Money is my employee and is here to serve me.
- I am always expecting the best for myself.
- I make wise investment choices that bring more and more money to invest.
- I allow unlimited prosperity to flow to me everyday.
- I channel love and energy to everyone around me.

- Money comes easily and effortlessly; I am a good receiver.
- I love to share and it brings me joy.
- I think and speak positively. I focus on what is good. I refuse to fear or dwell on the negative.
- I can accomplish anything I set my mind on.
- I delight in You, Lord, and You give me the desires of my heart.
- God provides and supplies all needs for me and all humanity.
- I am grateful for all the abundance I receive and the lifestyle I live.
- I give thanks for ever increasing health, youth and beauty.
- I am responsible for my own attitude.
- I expect lavish abundance every day in every way in my life and affairs.
- Wealth and abundance comes to me naturally!
- This is God's day, a good day. I pronounce this day and all of its activities good!
- Everyday I am increasing my wealth.
- I see every opportunity that comes my way.

The Last Word...

We have poured our heart and soul into each of these pages sharing the principles of self-mastery, and it all begins with making the decision to live more abundantly. So decide to change the way you feel today and you can then change the life you live. You can start shining your positive energy more brightly, you can feel what is going right in your life, and you can begin to feel confident and worthy of happiness, joy and inner peace.

Now, the only thing standing between you and success is your application of the principles bestowed within this book and the willingness to allow time to move you forward! On your journey, make sure you take time to celebrate every little success even if you are the only one who notices it.

We believe in you! We believe you have it within you to accomplish anything your heart desires. You will need to stay focused and disciplined to do it; if you came this far, there is no turning back.

Deborah Francis
Co-Founder, COO
Built To Prosper Companies
www.BuiltToProsperCompanies.com

Hasheem Francis
Co-Founder, CEO
Built To Prosper Companies
www.BuiltToProsperCompanies.com

BIBLIOGRAPHY

Francis, Deborah and Francis, Hasheem **Cashology: The Science Of Living A CASH ONLY Life**. Plymouth, FL.: BTP Publishing Group, 2010.

Francis, Hasheem. **Built To Prosper For Men: The 9 Principles of Self-Mastery**. Plymouth, FL.: BTP Publishing Group, 2011.

Baines, John. **The Secret Science**.: John Baines Institute, 1994.

Francis, Deborah **The Joy of Healthy Living, Without Your Health You Cannot Enjoy Your Wealth**. Plymouth, FL.: The Joy of Healthy Living, LLC , 2011.

Haanel, Charles. F. **The Master Key System**. St. Louis: Psychology Publishing, 1916.

Hill, Napoleon **Think and Grow Rich**. New York, NY: Penguin, 2008.

Thompson, Leroy, Dr. **Money Cometh: To The Body of Christ**. Darrow, LA: Ever Increasing Word Ministries, 1999.

Thompson, Leroy, Dr. **I'll Never Be Broke Another Day in My Life**. Darrow, LA: Ever Increasing Word Ministries, 2001.

Wattles, Wallace. D. **The Science Of Getting Rich**. New York: Elizabeth Towne Company, 1910.

Wattles, Wallace. D. **The Science Of Being Well**. New York: Elizabeth Towne Company, 1910.

ABOUT THE AUTHORS
Deborah Francis & Hasheem Francis

Deborah Francis is the COO and President of Built To Prosper Companies. Deborah is an entrepreneur, best-selling author, investor, keynote speaker, recognized industry thought leader, and an expert on business development. She has developed curriculums and delivered training sessions on entrepreneurship, small business development, and professional development. Deborah has trained, led, and mentored hundreds of people with her functional knowledge and educational background. Deborah has a Masters in Secondary Education of English. Deborah's focus is toward helping others master their lives by planning their destiny. She knows that empowerment resides in the minds of those who seek solutions and put them into action.

Hasheem Francis is the Chairman and CEO of Built To Prosper Companies. Hasheem is an entrepreneur, investor, best-selling author, keynote speaker, recognized industry thought leader, and an expert on executive business and leadership development. With two decades of entrepreneurial and leadership experience, Hasheem is a leadership consultant and advisor to CEOs, business leaders, corporate executives, and community leaders across the country.

RECOMMENDED READING LIST

Spiritual Life

1. The Bible
2. The Laws of Thinking – Bishop E. Bernard Jordan
3. Prayer of Jabez – Bruce Wilkerson
4. God's Creative Power – Charles Capp
5. Financial Prosperity – Kenneth Copeland
6. The Marked Bible – Charles L. Taylor
7. Enemy Access Denied – John Bevere
8. The Power of Praying Together – Stormie Omartian
9. Every Man's Battle – Stephen Arterburn
10. The Prideful Soul's Guide to Humility – Michael Fontenot & Thomas Jones
11. The Ultimate Gift – Jim Stovall
12. Some Sat in Darkness – Mike Leatherwood
13. Life on the High Wire – Martin Camp
14. The Greatest Salesman in the World – Og Mandino
15. Become a Better You – Joel Osteen
16. The Science of Love – John Baine
17. 24 Keys that Bring Complete Success – Paul J. Meyer
18. Loose That Man & Let Him Go – T.D Jakes
19. How to Find Your Wealthy Place – Dr. Leroy Thompson
20. Secret Ingredients for Spiritual Growth – Dr. Robert Kennedy
21. Framing Your World – Dr. Leroy Thompson
22. Battlefield of the Mind – Joyce Meyers
23. 8 Steps to Create the Life You Want – Creflo Dollar
24. You Were Born for This – Bruce Wilkinson
25. The Everyday Visionary – Jesse Duplantis

Wealth

1. Cashology: The Science of Living A Cash Only Life – Hasheem Francis & Deborah Francis
2. You Were Born Rich – Bob Proctor
3. Commander of Covenant Wealth – Dr. Leroy Thompson
4. Money Cometh – Dr. Leroy Thompson
5. Protecting Your #1 Assets – Michael Lechter
6. Dynamic Laws of Prosperity – Catherine Ponder
7. Cashology – Hasheem Francis & Deborah Francis
8. The Wealth Magnet – Dr. Dolf De Roos
9. Why We Want You Rich – Donald Trump & Robert Kiyosaki
10. Rich Dad Poor Dad – Robert Kiyosaki
11. Think and Grow Rich – Napoleon Hill
12. The Secret to Attracting Money – Dr. Joe Vital
13. The Richest Man in Babylon – George S. Clason
14. Cashflow Quadrants – Robert Kiyosaki
15. The Master of Money – Rev Ike
16. Think Like a Billionaire – Scot Anderson
17. Multiple Streams of Income – Robert Allen
18. 21 Distinctions of Wealth – Peggy McColl
19. Million Dollar Mindset – James Arthur Ray
20. Billionaire Secrets to Success – Bill Bartmann
21. Secrets of the Millionaire Mind – T. Harv Eker
22. How Rich People Think – Steve Siebold
23. Prosperity – Charles Filmore
24. The Way to Wealth – Benjamin

Leadership

1. The Leadership Bible – John C. Maxwell
2. The Seven Habits of Highly Effective People – Stephen R. Covey
3. Developing the Leader Within You – John C. Maxwell
4. Lincoln on Leadership - Donald Phillips
5. Become the Leader You Were Meant to Be – Paul J. Meyer
6. Man of Steel & Velvet – Aubrey Andelin
7. Primal Leadership – Daniel Goleman, Richard Boyatzis & Annie McKee
8. The 21 Irrefutable Laws of Leadership – John C. Maxwell
9. The Leadership Pill – Ken Blanchard
10. Built to Prosper – Hasheem Francis
11. Awaken the Giant Within – Tony Robbins
12. Who Moved My Cheese? – Spencer Johnson
13. Corps Values – Zell Miller
14. Living at the Summit – Dr. Tom Hill with John & Elizabeth Gardner
15. The Art of Leadership – J. Donald Walters
16. The Pre Paid Legal Story – Harland Stonecipher
17. How to Build a Large Organization – Paul J. Meyer
18. Extreme Dreams Depend on Teams – Pat Williams
19. A Leader in the Making – Joyce Meyers
20. Message of a Master – John McDonald
21. TNT: The Power Within You – Claude Bristol
22. The Leadership Challenge – James Kouzes
23. The Five Dysfunctions of a Team – Patrick Lencioni
24. Good to Great – Jim Collins

Marriage & Family

1. The Bible
2. The Power of a Praying Wife – Stormie Omartian
3. Friends & Lovers – Sam & Geri Laing
4. The Power of Praying Together – Stormie Omartian
5. Love Your Husband – Gloria Baird
6. Smart Couples Finish Rich – David Bach
7. Every Man's Battle – Stephen Arterburn
8. Love Dare – Stephen Kendrick
9. The Five Love Languages, Men's Edition – Steve Shores
10. The Purpose Driven Life – Rick Warren
11. The Science of Love – John Baine
12. The Five Languages of Love – Gary D. Chapman
13. You Can Heal Your Life – Louise Hay
14. Wake Up the Mighty Men – Darlene Bishop
15. Courtship After Marriage – Zig Ziglar
16. Family Promises – Kenneth Copeland
17. The Power of a Praying Husband – Stormie Omartian
18. The Discipline Book – Dr. Sears
19. The Man in the Mirror- Patrick Morley
20. The Power of a Praying Parent – Stormie Omartian
21. Grooming the Next Generation – Dani Johnson
22. The Power of Prayer to Change Your Marriage – Stormie Omartian
23. How to Put Your Family Under the Anointing – Dr. Leroy Thompson

Health
1. The Seven Pillars of Health – Dr. Don Colbert
2. The Science of Being Well – Wallace D. Wattles
3. Natural Health, Natural Medicine – Andrew Weil
5. The Joy of Healthy Living – Deborah Francis
6. Eat This and Live – Dr. Don Colbert
7. Live in the Divine Health – Dr. Don Colbert
8. What You Don't Know May Be Killing You – Dr. Don Colbert
9. Toxic Relief – Dr. Don Colbert
10. Platinum Workout – LL Cool J
11. Mind/Body Nutrition - Marc David
12. The Flex Brain Method – Nightingale Learning System
13. I Can Do This Diet – Dr. Don Colbert
14. Look Great, Feel Great – Joyce Meyers
15. Eat to Live – Joel Fuhrman
16. Change Your Habits, Change Your Life – Danna Demetre
17. Live Long, Finish Strong – Gloria Copeland
18. Billy's Ultimate Bootcamp – Billy Blanks
19. The Everything Family Nutrition Book – Leslie Bilderback
20. Prime Time Health – William Sears M.D

This is by no means a complete list of valuable resources for health. Criteria for picking appropriate literature include: quality of language and quality of principles taught within the book.

Children's Books
1. Dr. Seuss's Collection of Stories – Dr. Seuss
2. Fairy Tale Collection – Hans Christian Anderson
3. Uncle Arthur's Bedtime Stories – Arthur Stanley Maxwell
4. The Secret Garden – Frances Hodgson Burnett
5. A Little Princess – Frances Hodgson Burnett
6. Little Lord Fauntleroy – Frances Hodgson Burnett
7. The Little House Books – Laura Ingalls Wilder (9 total)
8. Little Women – Louisa May Alcott
9. Little Men – Louisa May Alcott
10. Eight Cousins – Louisa May Alcott
11. Rose in Bloom – Louisa May Alcott
12. Swiss Family Robinson – Johann Weiss
13. Black Beauty – Anna Sewell
14. Heidi – Johanna Spyri
15. To Kill a Mockingbird – Harper Lee
16. Jane Eyre – Charlotte Bronte
17. The Tenant of Wildfell Hall – Anne Bronte
18. Mansfield Park – Jane Austen
19. The Chronicles of Narnia – C.S. Lewis (7 total)
20. Kidnapped – Robert Louis Stevenson
21. The Princess and the Goblin – George Macdonald
22. The Princess and Curdie – George Macdonald
23. Clotel, or the President's Daughter – William Wells Brown
24. Uncle Tom's Cabin – Harriet Beecher Stowe
25. Walden – Henry David Thoreau

This is by no means a complete list of valuable resources for children.
All Children books were suggested by Kelly Steinruck

Notes

Notes

Notes

Notes

www.ingramcontent.com/pod-product-compliance
Lightning Source LLC
Chambersburg PA
CBHW061302110426
42742CB00012BA/2019